Rocketbone's Guide to North Korea

by J.R. JaBone

Illustrated by Zulfikar Rachman

CONTENTS

WELCOME!

Hi! My name is Rocketbone, an inter-galactic explorer from the planet P3T0N. Under orders from my commanders, I have been flying around outer-space searching for potential life on distant planets.

After years of disappointment, I spotted a blue and green orb floating in the distance near a star named Sol. What I thought would be a quick report has turned out to be anything but. This small planet is divided into 195 countries, each with its own unique people, flora, fauna, language, culture, government, and traditions.

Join me as I spend the next few years documenting my adventures on this sphere, whose inhabitants call Earth. My first stop, the Hermit Kingdom of North Korea!

Your Friend,

Rocketbone

CHAPTER 1

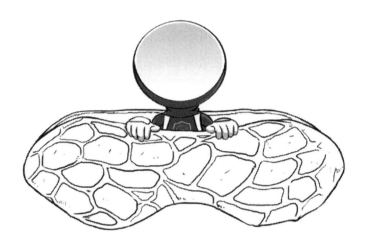

IN A NUTSHELL

Founded:	September 9, 1948
Capital:	Pyongyang
Population:	23 million
Official Name:	Democratic People's Republic of Korea (DPRK)
Nickname:	The Hermit Kingdom
Official Language:	Korean
Supreme Leader:	Kim Jong-un
National Symbol:	Chollima
National Tree:	Pine Tree
National Flower:	Oyama Magnolia

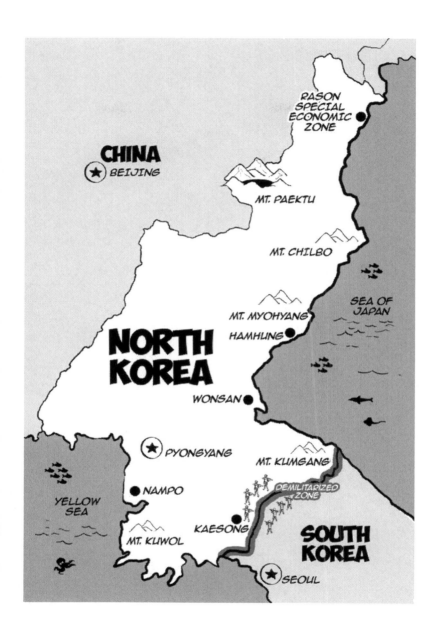

CHAPTER 2

GETTING THERE

Visiting North Korea is a little more complicated than just booking a flight. Unlike most other countries, there are restrictions and hurdles one must overcome to be allowed entrance into the Hermit Kingdom.

Visas

Applying for visas to North Korea is relatively easy compared to other countries. Your tour company (and you can only visit North Korea via a registered tour company) will help you through the process. Citizens of several countries including China, Cuba, Russia, and Switzerland are able to visit without a visa.

Currently, citizens of the United States and South Korea are not permitted to visit North Korea due to several incidents you will read about in later chapters.

Via Plane

Beijing, China is the typical starting point for any aerial trip to North Korea. From Beijing, you can take an Air Koryo flight to Pyongyang International Airport (North Korea's only international airport).

Via Train

A train journey allows travelers to pass through the North Korean border in a scenic way. The train is mostly ridden by middle-class citizens, as opposed to the more affluent ones who can afford the luxury of air travel. Expect to share a small cabin consisting of four beds, and although meals are included, it would be wise to bring snacks as the food isn't the most appetizing.

If starting in Beijing, expect this journey to take 24 hours. If a long train journey isn't for you, shorten your ride by catching the train near the border at Dandong, China, where it is about an eight-hour trip into Pyongyang.

Choosing A Tour Company

Tours range from two to 30 days. If solo travel is more of your thing, look into booking a private tour with one of the companies listed below. Just know that there will always be at least two government officials accompanying you on your journey.

Young Pioneer Tours

Founded in 2008 and based in China, Young Pioneer Tours is one of the most popular tour agencies for visiting North Korea as well as many other less-frequented countries, including Afghanistan and Turkmenistan.

Koryo Tours

Offering both group and private tours, Koryo is also very active in the North Korean film scene. They are responsible for coordinating the Pyongyang International Film Festival and producing North Korean feature films, including the critically acclaimed *Comrade Kim Goes Flying.*

Uri Tours

Unlike other places around the world you may visit, most tours in North Korea don't allow the time or space to stretch your legs and get some strenuous exercise in. Uri Tours, however, offers many specialty trips, geared around bicycling, surfing, and snowboarding

CHAPTER 3

HISTORY

The history of the small peninsula of Korea is dense enough to fill thousands of pages. For the sake of brevity, this section will focus on the highlights, from the days of the old Kingdoms to the turbulent events that have transpired over the past century.

Dawn of Civilization – 1945

Civilization in Korea dates back as far as 4000 BC, when farmers began to cultivate the land with stone age tools. Small tribes evolved into large kingdoms, and by 18 BC there were three, the Silla, Goryeo, and Baekje. The Silla emerged as the dominant kingdom and united Korea around 700 AD.

From the years 700 to 1592 AD, Korea was invaded again and again. First the Mongols came, and savagely tried to make Korea their own. After eventually fighting them off, the Koreans were introduced to Confucius philosophy by their Chinese neighbors. Entering an age of enlightenment, they built extravagant temples and created beautiful pottery.

In 1656, Koreans were introduced to European culture for the first time when a ship from the Netherlands shipwrecked on their shore. Koreans were influenced by Western religion, and many converted to Catholicism.

The doors would shut in 1800, as Korea adopted an isolationist policy. Bearing resemblance to the North Korea of today, trade and contact with foreigners was forbidden. In 1886, French priests attempting to spread their religious views were executed by Korean soldiers, and an American war ship was bombed off the shores of Korea in 1871.

The Industrial Revolution of the late 1800's would pressure Korea to abandon their isolationist approach. They signed peace treaties with the United States and France, as well as Japan, a country that would soon betray them.

Japan, an economic and military power during this period, began to increasingly interfere with Korean affairs. Soon Japan would take control, disbanding the Korean military in 1907, and then officially annexing the entire country of Korea in 1910.

The Japanese pressured Koreans to adopt Japanese names, speak the Japanese language, and convert to Shinto-Buddhism, the most popular religion in Japan. When the

Koreans peacefully protested, the Japanese arrested or executed them. Korea was losing its identity to the Japanese.

World War II began, and many Koreans were sent to the front lines to fight on behalf of the Japanese. Others were forced into manual labor at wartime factories. After a long and bloody war, Japan would be defeated by the tag team of the United States and Soviet Union, finally freeing Korea from the Japanese occupation.

1945 – Present

With their defeat in World War II, Japan no longer ruled Korea. The Americans and Soviets decided that Korea would be the spoils of their victory over Japan. Although they worked as a team during World War II, ideologically the two countries could not be more different. The Soviets preached communism and totalitarianism, giving all power to the rulers, while the United States promoted capitalism and democracy.

Rather than fight over these philosophical differences, they agreed to divide Korea at the 38th parallel, the Soviets getting the north and the Americans the south. The Soviets would install the young, charismatic war hero Kim Il-sung as their new leader, while the Americans appointed anti-communist leader Syngman Rhee.

Over time, the political and philosophical differences between the North and the South would lead to conflict. Both leaders would claim the whole of Korea, creating tension that would lead to the North invading the South and sparking the Korean War in 1950.

The United Nations came to the aid of South Korea, while China and the Soviet Union would help out North Korea. After three years of fighting and two-and-a-half million casualties, North and South Korea signed an armistice agreement in July of 1953. Fighting would cease, the territory would remain the same, and a high security Demilitarized Zone (DMZ) would be constructed along the border.

Following the Korean War, North Korea, under Kim Il-sung, established the Juche Ideology, which promoted self-reliance upon its citizens. Private property was abolished, and the media became state-controlled.

The Soviet Union would continue to support North Korea, acting as a big brother for the next few decades. In fact, for a long period, the North's economy and living conditions were far superior to that of the impoverished, post war South, which was supported by the United States and organizations such as the Peace Corps.

Unfortunately for Kim Il-sung, big brother would collapse. The Soviet Union disbanded in 1992, and North Korea was left with China as their strongest international ally. Trade, and in turn resources, became limited.

Kim Il-sung died of a heart attack in 1994, leaving the nation grieving. His son, Kim Jong-il, would succeed him, and preside over the darkest time in Korean history.

Flooding and poor agricultural policies, as well as the loss of support from the Soviets, led to a famine which killed hundreds of thousands of citizens. Government travel restrictions meant that citizens had nowhere to go. Those who tried to escape were sent to work camps or executed. South Korea, Japan, the United States, and several other countries eventually came to the aid of the North Koreans, and by 1998 the worst of the famine was over.

The start of the new millennium was bright, as peace talks were ongoing with United States Secretary of State Madeline Albright. A train station near the DMZ was even constructed for eventual travel between the two Koreas. Unfortunately, it was revealed that North Korea has been secretly testing nuclear weapons. Peace talks ended and the soon to be opened train station stood empty.

In the wake of the terrorist attacks of September 11, 2001, former American President George W. Bush named North Korea as one of the countries in the "Axis of Evil". On October 9, 2006, North Korea conducted their first successful nuclear test. From that point on North and South Korea have appeared to be on the brink of war.

In December of 2011, Kim Jong-il died of a heart attack. His enigmatic 27-year-old son, Kim Jong-un, was chosen to take the reins of this mysterious, isolationist, and dangerous nation.

In subsequent years, Kim Jong-un would execute anyone who crossed him. Many members of the government were executed, including his own uncle. Nuclear tests were also on the rise. After testing weapons that they claimed were stronger than the atomic bomb, tensions between North Korea and the United States increased to an all-time high.

War seemed inevitable after a series of threatening tweets and speeches between United States President Donald Trump and Kim Jong-un in 2017. Cooler heads prevailed, thankfully, and the two leaders decided to meet in Singapore. The meeting ended in a handshake, and although future peace summits are in the works, the future of North Korea is as uncertain as ever.

CHAPTER 4

THE THREE KIMS

KIM IL-SUNG (1912-1994)
ETERNAL PRESIDENT

The Kims aren't Kings. However, throughout the country's 71-year history, a member of the Kim dynasty has constantly been in power. Historians call this a hereditary dictatorship.

Born in Mangyondae, a suburb of Pyongyang, Kim Il-sung and his family escaped the Japanese occupation and fled to Northeast China when he was just a small boy. In China, he joined an organization of youth communists and became entranced with their philosophy.

He returned to Korea in the 1930s and united a group of resistance guerillas intent on ending the Japanese occupation. His war strategy and brave tactics endeared him to the long-suffering Korean people.

During World War II, he became a Major in the Soviet Army. Following the war, the Soviets appointed him the first leader of the newly formed North Korea at the age of 36.

In 1950, with the aid of his Soviet Allies, Il-sung ordered an invasion of South Korea under the guise of reunification. South Korea, with the help of the United States and the United Nations, fought back until the two sides reached a stalemate, ending the Korean War in 1953.

Following the war, Il-sung introduced the Juche philosophy. Juche, representing the idea of self-reliance, propelled North Korea into a period of isolationism that would last until the present time.

Although Kim Il-sung passed away in 1994, he is still considered North Korea's eternal president.

KIM JONG-IL (1941-2011)
ETERNAL GENERAL SECRETARY

Kim Jong-il, the son of Kim Il-sung, was born February 16, 1941. Details of his birth are heavily disputed. While it is generally accepted that his mother was living in Siberia (modern day Russia) during the time of his birth, the North Korean government states that he was born under a double rainbow at a guerrilla fighter base camp on Mount Paektu.

As the son of the leader of North Korea, Jong-il lived the life of a privileged youth. In Pyongyang, he was trained in the art of propaganda and became the Worker's Party Secretary.

An avid film lover, Jong-il reportedly owned a collection of more than 20,000 movies. He authored books on the art of cinema, kidnapped South Korean directors to produce North Korean films, and even produced and directed some of his own films.

According to North Korean state-run media, Jong-il was also a legendary athlete. In his first game of golf, he allegedly shot four hole-in-ones. During his first game of bowling, he scored a perfect 300. These seemingly impossible feats, much like his birthplace, continue to raise doubts.

After his father's death, Jong-il became North Korea's second leader with the title of Chairman. The infamous famine of the mid-1990's made his first years in office truly trying. His legacy as a leader is overshadowed by numerous complaints of human rights violations. Unsanctioned nuclear tests further isolated North Korea from their neighbors, as well as taking them to the brink of war with the United States.

Jong-il, who had a lifetime fear of flying, died of a heart attack while on his train in 2011. Posthumously the government declared him their eternal General Secretary.

KIM JONG-UN (1984-)
CHAIRMAN

The youngest of Jong-il's three sons, Kim Jong-un's childhood is shrouded in mystery. He was schooled in the Swiss capital of Bern, where classmates described him as quiet with a high interest in basketball.

After graduating in Switzerland, he returned to Pyongyang where he served in the North Korean State Department under his father and became a four-star General. Following his father's sudden death, Jong-un was appointed leader of North Korea at the youthful age of 27.

Since taking over for his father, he has kept quite an eccentric lifestyle. He has become friendly with American basketball stars and even created his own pop band, Moranbong. According to his former private chef, Jong-un's favorite band is The Beatles and his favorite actor is Jean Claude Van Dam.

Under Jong-un, North Korea claims they have found a cure for the HIV and Ebola viruses, as well as discovering a secret unicorn lair in Pyongyang. However, Jong-un has also become a ruthless leader, executing several members of the North Korean government, including his own uncle.

CHAPTER 5

THE DMZ

Stretching 160 miles long and two and a half miles wide, the Demilitarized Zone (DMZ) is unlike anywhere else on Earth. It is a stretch of land laden with over 1.2 million landmines, wild animals, surveillance cameras, barbed wire, electric fencing, ghostly villages, and soldiers on either side prepared to start World War III given enough provocation.

In 1953, following the conclusion of the Korean War, North and South Korea agreed to build the DMZ along the 38th parallel. In reality, there are three borders. The North Korean Border, the Military Demarcation Line (MDL), and the South Korean Border. Soldiers from the North and South are only allowed to cross the MDL with special permission.

The most well-known area of the DMZ, and perhaps the image that comes to most people's mind, is the Joint Security Area (JSA). The JSA is the spot where military personnel from North and South Korea (with United States reinforcements) face each other. It is also the place where diplomatic meetings between the North and South take place.

Located in the village of Panmunjom, the JSA contains several buildings. Most famous are the Phanmun Pavilion (North Korea), and the House of Freedom (South Korea/United Nations). These two multi-level buildings face each other, with several blue smaller buildings in between designated for negotiations.

Villages Within the DMZ

The creation of the DMZ affected many people in Korea. Friends and families who had been separated by a few miles of grassy fields were now separated by armed soldiers and landmines. Some unfortunate villages were actually trapped inside the DMZ.

Kijong-dong, also known as "Propaganda Village", is located on the North Korean side of the DMZ. It is famous for its 525-foot flagpole, the fourth largest in the world. Approximately 200 citizens live here, according to the North Korean government, although most anyone who has seen this village would certainly dispute this (you can look down at the empty village through binoculars from the South Korean side).

Besides the flagpole, Kijong-dong is famous for its loudspeakers that preach North Korean propaganda for up to 20 hours a day at a volume loud enough to be heard in South Korea.

Not to be outdone, Daeseong-dong is the only inhabited village in the DMZ on the South Korean side. Their flagpole, at a height of 323 feet, pales in comparison to their northern neighbor. The only citizens permitted to live there are those who resided there before the creation of the DMZ. The loudspeakers from this village blast Korean pop songs, typically from all-girl bands. For their protection, all 226 residents must be home by 11:00 PM every night for a headcount, and wear ID badges at all times.

Animals of the DMZ

To say that nature at the DMZ is well preserved would be an understatement. With no tourists, no highways, and very little pollution, animal populations have thrived. As a result, the DMZ is home to over 300 species of birds, as well as dangerous carnivores like bears, leopards, and tigers.

Tunnels

Four tunnels have been discovered by South Korean officials since 1974. They believe the tunnels, placed in different strategic spots along the DMZ, were constructed for a planned invasion of the South. The North denies this, claiming they were used for coal mining. Today, South Korean tour agencies offer tours to three of the four tunnels.

DMZ Incidents

The DMZ was supposed to be a neutral zone in which meetings could be held to settle conflicts peacefully between the North and the South. Instead, its history is one of infiltrations, escapes, and violence. Descriptions of the most notable follow.

Korean DMZ Conflict (1966-1969)

Also known as the Second Korean War, this conflict consisted of many different small battles, attacks, and assassination attempts. In total, 397 North Koreans, 299 South Koreans, and 43 Americans lost their lives during this violent period.

On New Year's Day 1968, the Blue House Raid occurred. The Blue House, home to then South Korean President Park Chung-hee, is South Korea's version of the White House. A team of 31 North Korean soldiers, disguised as South Korean soldiers, snuck past the DMZ intent on killing Chung-hee. They made it all the way to the Blue House, where finally they were confronted by real South Korean soldiers. A firefight ensued, leaving 28 of the 31 North Koreans dead, as well as killing 26 South Korean and three American soldiers.

Axe Murder Incident (1976)

If this incident sounds gory and gruesome, well, it is. Things were relatively quiet on a warm summer day at the DMZ. A huge poplar tree, however, was about to cause one of the tensest moments ever in DMZ history.

The poplar tree was big and growing bigger, causing the United States' and South Korea's view of the military checkpoints to be obscured. The solution, they thought, was to trim the tree. On August 18, 1976, American soldiers, with the aid of South Korean soldiers, drove to the tree and began trimming.

Shortly after, North Korean soldiers arrived, telling the Americans they must stop. They claimed the tree was planted by none other than Kim Il-sung and held great significance to the people of North Korea. The Americans shrugged and continued to trim. Tensions escalated and finally a North Korean commander shouted, "kill them!" In less than a minute, two American soldiers were bludgeoned to death with axes.

North Korea released a statement saying the killings were in self-defense. Meanwhile, at the Pentagon, the United States began planning a retaliation. Operation Paul Bunyan would be the name of this mission, and chopping the tree down would be the primary objective.

On August 21, 1976, American soldiers returned to the tree. This time, they brought 16 men with chainsaws. In case of retaliation, they had tanks aiming at North Korea, as well as helicopters and B-52 bombers ready at a moment's notice. It is rumored that these bombers contained nuclear weapons. As if that wasn't enough, the battleship USS Midway was waiting off the shores of Wonsan, North Korea, as well as thousands of troops in nearby Okinawa, Japan.

Fortunately, these reinforcements were not needed. The tree was chopped down, and North Korea, for the only time in their history, gave a half-hearted apology accepting blame for their role in the deaths of the American soldiers. Today, a plaque memorializing the fallen troops stands in the spot where the tree stood.

Oh Chong-song's Escape (2017)

It is estimated that approximately 1,000 North Koreans escape to South Korea each year. However, it is extremely rare for them to traverse the DMZ, especially in the JSA. On November 13, 2017, North Korean soldier Oh Chong-song drove his jeep past border patrols along the MDL, before jumping out and running across to South Korea and safety. His North Korean comrades shot at him, getting five successful shots in. With the aid of United States and South Korean soldiers, Chong-song was nursed back to health. He currently lives in South Korea.

Trump Crosses the DMZ (2019)

On June 30, 2019, President Trump stunned the world, becoming the first sitting United States president to step foot inside the Hermit Kingdom. On the north side of the JSA, Trump and Kim Jong-un shook hands and had a private meeting with South Korean President Moon Jae-in. While details of this meeting aren't entirely public, all parties said the meeting went well, with Trump extending an invitation for Kim Jong-un to visit the White House.

CHAPTER 6

PYONGYANG

Pyongyang is the capital of North Korea, home to many of the country's most iconic monuments and museums. It is believed that only those citizens who best exemplify the Juche philosophy are permitted to live here.

Even though its population is officially listed at 3.2 million, there is very little automobile traffic and crime is virtually non-existent. The cleanliness and modernity of Pyongyang will astound you, although it is important to remember that not all of North Korea is like this.

PLACES TO SEE

Arc de Triumph

If the Arc de Triumph looks familiar, then you have probably been to Paris, France. At 200 feet tall, it is 33 feet taller than its Parisian counterpart and with significantly less traffic running through it. Kim Il-sung ordered its construction in 1982 to commemorate the Korean Resistance to Japan, and it has been an iconic symbol of Pyongyang ever since.

Pyongyang Metro

While the streets of Pyongyang are among the emptiest of any capital city in the world, beneath the streets it is a different story. Opened in 1973, the Pyongyang Metro has only two lines and 16 stops total, and costs only five won (less than a penny) to ride. Doubling as a bomb shelter, this subway system lies 350 feet below North Korea's capital. The stations are quite ornate, with chandeliers hanging from the ceiling and murals adorning the walls. Every subway car displays portraits of the two deceased Kims watching over.

Kumusan Palace of the Sun

The Palace of the Sun is one of the holiest and most emotional places one can visit on a trip to North Korea. In most countries, former leaders are buried in grandiose cemeteries. This is not the case in North Korea. Kim Il-sung and his son, Kim Jong-il, are both displayed, perfectly preserved, in a glass case (think *Sleeping Beauty*) for citizens to come and pay their respects.

Built in 1976, the temple was the official residence of Kim Il-sung until his death in 1994. The temple feels like an airport, as one must ride miles of people-movers just to reach the security lobby. You are not allowed to bring any items inside temple grounds. Wallets, cameras, phones, and even watches are strictly forbidden. Talking while inside is also prohibited.

Juche Tower

The Juche Tower is located just beside the Taedong River in Central Pyongyang. It was built to honor the founder of Juche, Kim Il-sung, on his 70th birthday. At the base of this monumental obelisk are dozens of small plaques from students of Juche from all over the world, proving that this philosophy is not exclusive to North Korea. An elevator lets visitors ascend to an outdoor platform beneath a glowing eternal flame, providing 360-degree views of the Pyongyang skyline.

Korean Central Zoo

The Korean Central Zoo is home to over 5,000 animals from 600 different species. While you're more likely to come across a dog on a plate than in a street in Pyongyang, the zoo is one place where you can find our furry four-legged friend.

Most of the animals in the zoo are said to be gifts from foreign diplomats. Perhaps the most bizarre animal on display is a chimpanzee named Azalea, who is famous for smoking a pack of cigarettes a day. While most zoos around the world are constantly evolving to take a more humane approach towards animal captivity, this particular zoo seems to be headed in the opposite direction.

Department Store Number One

In most countries around the world, a department store wouldn't exactly qualify as a tourist attraction. Years of urban legends, reinforced by the depiction of a phony supermarket in the movie *The Interview*, have led many foreigners to believe that real department stores do not exist in North Korea.

Located in the heart of Pyongyang, Department Store Number One is one of the only places where foreigners can shop freely, side by side, with citizens of Pyongyang.

While the book stores, stamp shops, and other souvenir retailers are usually empty (except for tour groups), this store is often crammed with long lines of locals waiting to check out. With three floors of food, clothing, toys, alcohol, electronics, bags, and a fourth-floor food court, one can spend hours there.

This is also one of the few places where you can obtain North Korean won currency. There is an exchange booth at the front of the store, and after making your purchases, you are expected to exchange your remaining won back to euros or dollars. It is illegal to bring won out of North Korea, however many foreigners do it as a way of keeping a unique souvenir.

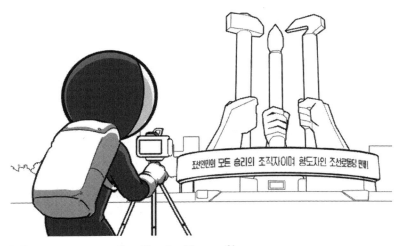

Monument to the Party Founding

Rising 160 feet into the air in the middle of Pyongyang is a giant granite monument of the proletariat. The Monument to the Party Founding, as it is known, was built in 1995 to commemorate the 50-year anniversary of the Worker's Party.

Three fists hold tools symbolic of the working class; a hammer to represent the workers, a sickle to represent the farmers, and a paint brush to represent the intellectuals. A quote stating "Long live the Workers Party of Korea, which organizes and guides all victories for the Korean people!" is located at the base of the monument.

Arch of Reunification

Someday there will be a highway from Seoul, the capital of South Korea, to Pyongyang. When that happens, vehicles will pass beneath the Arch of Reunification. The Arch was built in August of 2001 and stands over 200 feet tall. The arch is connected by twin statues of traditionally dressed Korean women holding a unified map of Korea.

Pyongyang Traffic Ladies

In many intersections on the not-so-busy streets of Pyongyang and other North Korean cities, you will find the immaculately dressed, authoritative "traffic ladies". Dressed in high heels, skirts, and blue police tops, these women are said to be chosen by the government largely for their good looks. They hold one of the most elite civil positions in Pyongyang and have been featured on everything from stamps to dolls. While there are more than 50 traffic ladies working in Pyongyang alone, the recent implementation of traffic lights throughout the capital threaten their future.

Ryugyong Hotel

The Ryugyong Hotel looks like something out of a futuristic science fiction movie, although its history is very much stuck in the past. Work on this stunning pyramid-shaped hotel began in 1987, however, due to the economic crisis and famine of the 1990's, construction has stalled.

Today, what would have been the tallest hotel in the world in the 1990's now has the dubious honor of being the tallest unoccupied building in the world. Nonetheless, the Ryugyong is a majestic example of neo-futurist architecture, and a definite metaphor for the hopes and struggles of the North Korean people.

Victorious War Museum/USS Pueblo

The Victorious War Museum in Pyongyang celebrates North Korea's "victory" over the South and its allies in the Korean War. On display are dozens of bombed-out and captured American planes, tanks, and helicopters. Inside the museum's many levels are gruesome depictions of North Korea's battle victories. In one particular diorama, mannequins of lifeless American and Australian soldiers are surrounded by hovering vultures.

A 360-degree panoramic painting, complete with sound and light effects, allows visitors to immerse themselves in the Battle of Taejon.

Outside the museum sits the USS Pueblo. The Pueblo, a United States Navy spy ship, was attacked and captured on January 23, 1968, resulting in one American death.

For 11 months, American naval officers were held hostage. North Korea demanded an apology and confession of wrongdoing, and on December 23 of that year, all 83 hostages were released. The empty ship remains a trophy for North Korea, and visitors are allowed inside to watch a short documentary film and learn more.

Chollima Statue

From an unassuming tourist's perspective, the Chollima Statue might appear to just be a statue of a woman and a man riding a horse. However, the statue symbolizes much more than that. The Chollima is a mythical winged horse that is able to fly up to 300 miles in a single day. Kim Il-sung used the Chollima to inspire his people to achieve greatness by pushing themselves beyond their physical and mental limits for the betterment of their country. The statue was designed by the Mansudae Art Studio, responsible for nearly all statues and monuments nationwide. It was unveiled on April 15, 1961, Kim Il-sung's 49th birthday.

Taedongmoon Cinema House

This majestic movie theatre dates back to 1955 and is the most famous in the country. With two enormous screens, Taedongmoon Cinema House is also home to the

Pyongyang International Film Festival. If possible, ask your guide to see a movie here. Classics such as *The Flower Girl* and *Pulgasari* are often shown here.

Choson Film Studios

Just outside Pyongyang's city center is the very place where most North Korean films are produced, the Choson Film Studio. These studios have sets designed to resemble places in China, Japan, Europe, and even Ancient Korea.

Founded in 1947, a visit here provides insight into the propaganda machine, while also giving movie buffs a rare glimpse inside one of the most prolific studios in all of Asia.

Mansu Hill Grand Monument

The Mansu Hill Grand Monument is one of the most famous places in all of North Korea. The monument was originally built as a statue of Kim Il-sung. It was erected in April of

1972 to commemorate his 60th birthday.

After Kim Jong-il's death in 2011, a second statue was added. Both statues now stand side by side, with a beautiful mural of Mount Paektu as a backdrop. Standing over 66 feet tall, these statues symbolize the importance of these leaders to the North Korean people.

Visitors are expected to bow in reverence to the leaders upon visiting. As a sign of respect, they are also encouraged to buy and leave flowers, which can be purchased from nearby flower vendors.

PLACES TO EAT AND DRINK

Chongnyon Burger Restaurant

For fast food lovers, this might be the closest you'll come to having a Happy Meal. Choose between fast food staples such as burgers, fries, ice cream and coffee. Waffles and popcorn are also available here.

Italian Restaurant

If you enjoy Italian food, head over to Italian Restaurant. Yes, that's the official name of the restaurant housing North Korea's best pizza and most delicious pasta. It opened in December of 2009 after Kim Jong-il reportedly sent North Korean chefs to Naples and Rome to learn techniques from some of the most gifted Italian chefs.

KHC

Perhaps the best potato chips in all of North Korea, KHC is a small kiosk that serves up their own version of potato wedges in Kentucky Fried Chicken styled paper cartons. No one knows exactly what KHC stands for, but the chips are fantastic!

Number One Duck Barbeque

Tour groups typically enjoy their final meal here. Singing waitresses allow you to cook your own strips of duck on a simmering stove right at your table. For vegetarians, egg omelets and rice are available.

Okryu

The most famous restaurant in North Korea, Okryu is known for its long lines and cheap, delicious cold noodles. It is also a great place to people-watch. Adventurous foodies can try their other specialty, turtle soup.

Pyulmori Café

This café is modeled after European cafés. While its attempt at European cuisine is a complete fail, their coffee, although mediocre at best, is the best you'll find in the country.

Taedonggang Beer Bar

One of the most bustling spots in Pyongyang, Taedonggang is a great place to mingle with the most aristocratic crowds in Pyongyang. Here, it should be easy for you to exchange pleasantries over a beer with locals, ex-pats, and fellow tourists. With a selection of seven local beers, as well as delicious snacks (I highly recommend their dried fish and french fries), Taedonggang is worth visiting multiple times.

Taedonggang Seafood Restaurant

To call this place a restaurant is an injustice. This three-level seafood emporium is much more than that. The ground floor features various artificial ponds, loaded with salmon, sturgeon, trout, and various shellfish.

Using a net, you can select whichever fish you crave, and have it cooked for you upstairs. If catch and eat isn't your thing, sushi and all you can eat buffet options are also available. Opened in 2018, if this is a glimpse of the future of eateries in Pyongyang, one can be very excited.

The Yanggakdo Hotel Revolving Restaurant

I certainly don't recommend the food here, however, the 360-degree views make the dry chicken slightly more edible. It is a nice place to have a cold, refreshing drink on your first night in Pyongyang.

PLACES TO SLEEP

Koryo Hotel

Built in 1985, this 500-room hotel is 45 stories tall. While not the most modern hotel in Pyongyang, the Koryo Hotel boasts a cinema, conference halls, swimming pools, massage parlors, and many other amenities. Its close proximity to the train station makes it a strategic location for getting in, out, and around Pyongyang and neighboring cities.

Yanggakdo International Hotel

Built in 1995, this 47-floor, 1,000 room hotel is the perfect place to stay if you want to feel completely isolated from the rest of the world. Located on Yanggakdo Island in the middle of the Taedonggang River, this hotel almost feels like a cruise ship, with bowling lanes, karaoke, a bookshop, a hair salon, and an indoor pool.

For those looking for a little outdoor exercise, it is possible to walk around the hotel grounds without a government minder. Don't stray too far though!

CHAPTER 7

Hamhung	35 mi
Kaesong	67 mi
Nampo	120 mi
Rason	214 mi
Wonsan	268 mi

OTHER MAJOR CITIES

While most of the famous landmarks, museums, and historical sites are located in Pyongyang, one must not underestimate the number of things to experience outside the capital.

HAMHUNG

With over 750,000 residents, Hamhung is North Korea's second largest city. Like Pyongyang, it was nearly wiped off the map during the Korean War. For surfers and agricultural buffs, Hamhung is the place you want to be.

PLACES TO SEE

Hungnam Fertilizer Plant

Founded in 1929 during the Japanese occupation, Hungnam Fertilizer Plant employs over 7,300 workers, with over 35% of them being female. Serving as the principle manufacturer of all North Korean insecticides and fertilizers, this plant has also been suspected of manufacturing chemical weapons.

Tongbong Cooperative Farm

This village of approximately 1,000 farmers and their families is an exceptional place to visit. The living conditions of the workers, to the naked eye, are among the best you will see in North Korea. While you will be confronted with propaganda murals everywhere you turn, modern farming equipment and village shops filled with delicious local produce make Tongbong a delightful place to spend an afternoon.

The Hamhung Grand Theatre

Built in 1984 and containing over 800 rooms, this is the largest theatre in the country. It is located in Hamhung's Central Square. Enjoy a play or an opera inside or simply marvel outside at this colossal building.

Majon Beach

Just outside Hamhung, this beach is located in the Sea of Japan and is home to the Majon Surf School, one of the few places in the country where you can surf. The waves are perfect for all, from beginners to experts. If you are not a surfer, you can paddleboard, play volleyball, or join one of the nightly beachside bonfires.

PLACES TO EAT AND DRINK

Sinhunsang Noodle House

The must-eat treat of Hamhung is cold noodles. While Pyongyang-style is buckwheat noodles in a beef-broth, Hamhung-style is a delicious combination of sweet potato noodles in a peppery broth. Delicious!

PLACES TO SLEEP

Majon Hotel

The Majon Hotel, with a stunning private beach steps away from its front door, is one of the nicest hotels you will find in the Hermit Kingdom. Built in 2009, this hotel features 108 rooms, including some "first class" rooms complete with a living room and hot tub. Fall asleep to the sound of crashing waves and wake up to magnificent sunrises. If the ocean is too cold, go for a swim in their heated indoor pool.

KAESONG CITY

The capital of Korea from 918-1392, Kaesong is the closest major city to the South Korean border. Fans of ginseng can rejoice in a visit here, as Kaesong ginseng is widely considered the best in the world.

PLACES TO SEE

UNESCO Heritage Site: Monuments and Sites of Kaesong

This well-preserved archeological site, encompassing 12 major historical monuments in the vicinity of Kaesong, joined the Complex of Koguryo Tombs as the second UNESCO (United Nations Educational, Scientific and

Cultural Organization) heritage site in North Korea in 2013. Listed below are some must-sees.

Koryo Museum

Occupying a former school of Confucius Studies, this expansive museum houses over 1,000 relics from the Koryo dynasty. The ancient folk costumes, pottery, and original coffin from the tomb of King Kongmin are magnificent, as are the grounds, with 1,000-year-old gingko trees sheltering you from the sun. Be sure to stop at the gift shop here, as their selection of postcards and ginseng are among the best you'll find.

Sonjuk Bridge

The Sonjuk Bridge isn't famous for its practicality, but rather it's historical significance. This tiny stone bridge is only 17 feet in length, and crosses a shallow, narrow river that wouldn't be very intimidating to walk across.

On April 26, 1392, a revered Korean diplomat named Jeong Mong-ju was assassinated by five men with an iron hammer. Today, brown stains on the stones of the bridge are said to turn red when it rains, rumored to be the blood of Mong-ju.

Tomb of King Kongmin and Queen Noguk

The tale of King Kongmin is truly heartbreaking. Kongmin, a popular ruler of the Goryeo dynasty, desperately wanted an heir with his wife, the Mongolian-born Queen Noguk. After 15 years of trying, Noguk became pregnant. Sadly, neither the Queen nor the baby survived childbirth. A devastated Kongmin became indifferent to politics until his death.

Despite his political apathy, King Kongmin was very hands-on in the designing of his tomb. On top of a verdant, serene hill just outside Kaesong sits two burial mounds. A narrow underground passageway connects the two. In 1905, Japanese tomb-raiders broke into the tomb, stripping it of all the items the royal family had stored for the after-life.

Manwoldae Palace

Little remains of this former palace of the Goryeo Kingdom other than its stone foundation. Its location, however, amidst empty grasslands on the outskirts of Kaesong, provides travelers with some much-appreciated fresh air. Manwoldae translates into "hill for watching moon", and it is the ideal place for the locals of Kaesong to celebrate the Lunar New Year.

PLACES TO EAT AND DRINK

Tongil Restaurant

Usually packed with groups of foreigners either heading to or returning from the DMZ, Tongil Restaurant's fancy interior will make you feel as if you are about to attend a diplomatic banquet. A meal here includes namul, small bronze bowls filled with an assortment of meats and veggies. For an additional fee, you can order dog meat soup or the world-famous ginseng chicken.

PLACES TO SLEEP

Kaesong Folk Custom Hotel

Don't expect modern amenities at this throwback to old time traveling. The Kaesong Folk Custom Hotel features traditional style Korean homes. Accordingly, expect to eat and sleep on heated floors. Opened as a hotel in 1989, the structure dates back to the end of the 19th century.

<u>NAMPO</u>

Nampo is famous for its shipbuilding industry, the Nampo Dam, and local delicacies, such as gas clams. Nampo is also the closest port city to Pyongyang, and North Korea's biggest port on the Yellow Sea.

PLACES TO SEE

Nampo Dam

Also known as the West Sea Barrage, this dam is over four miles long and separates the Taedong River from the West Sea. It took only five years to build (1981-1986), which is a great source of pride for North Koreans. The dam was built to protect the inland from floods, although foreign critics speculate that the dam contributed to the famine of the 1990's. Today, you can visit the Nampo Dam Visitor Center, where you are encouraged to watch a short documentary celebrating this feat of engineering.

UNESCO Heritage Site: Complex of Koguryo Tombs

In 2004, the Complex of Koguryo Tombs became North Korea's first UNESCO World Heritage Site. Located in Kangso, between Pyongyang and Nampo, there are several beautifully preserved tombs to see.

Three Mausoleums of Kangso

Discovered by Japanese archaeologist Imanishi Ryu in 1911, this mausoleum is my favorite ruin in all of North Korea. Beautifully colored cave murals adorn the walls and give us a glimpse of what life was like during the days of the Koguryo Kingdom (300 BC to 700 AD).

It is believed that the tombs located here were made for kings, members of the royal family, and members of the aristocracy. Sixteen of the 63 tombs are adorned with wall paintings depicting the food, attire, religion, burial customs, and activities of the period.

There is also a mural of the four sacred animals of the ancient Kingdom; the blue dragon, white tiger, phoenix, and hanmu (a turtle shaped creature).

PLACES TO EAT AND DRINK

Pyongyang Mullet Soup Restaurant

The Pyongyang Mullet Soup Restaurant in downtown Nampo is worth visiting. The must-eat food in Nampo are the gas clams (see Chapter 16).

PLACES TO SLEEP

The Ryonggang Hot Spa Hotel

The popular Ryonggang Hot Spa Hotel is actually a series

of resort style villas each with their own private spa. The hotel is located in the peaceful countryside approximately 12 miles outside Nampo. You can enjoy karaoke or participate in a game of ping pong or billiards at the hotel. There is an on-site restaurant, and the 18-hole Thaesong Golf Course is easily accessible to hotel guests.

RASON SPECIAL ECONOMIC ZONE

On the Border of China and Russia sits the Rason Special Economic Zone. Established in 1992, it is an experimental area where some facets of capitalism are generally accepted. Its name is derived from two other cities, Rajin and Sonbong.

With three seaports, a direct train link to Russia, and a highway to China, Rason is a major business hub for both Chinese and Russian entrepreneurs.

The Uam Seal Sanctuary and the Rajin Shoe Factory provide unique experiences, while the Revolutionary Museum and pair of Kim statues are ubiquitously North Korean.

PLACES TO SEE

Golden Triangle Bank

In Rason, foreigners can spend North Korean currency freely. The Golden Triangle Bank, which towers seven stories above Rajin, allows foreigners to come in and open up their own bank accounts. You can even get your very own North Korean credit card!

PLACES TO EAT AND DRINK

The Fish Market

The stalls of the fish market offer some of the cheapest and most delicious seafood options you will find in Asia. You can choose from a vast selection of seafood including fresh fish, shrimp, and oysters.

Here, you can enjoy your food in the mayhem of the market, where unlike the rest of North Korea, you can watch shoppers haggle and negotiate with vendors for the best prices. There is also a Czech brewery and a Ukrainian restaurant if you feel compelled to take a break from Korean food.

PLACES TO SLEEP

Imperial Hotel

Built in 1999 by investors from Hong Kong, the Imperial Hotel is as close to a five-star hotel as you're going to find in North Korea.

Located on a quiet, serene beach outside of the city center, this palatial hotel is regularly filled with Chinese tourists, who like to spend the day gambling at the smoke-filled casino next door.

WONSAN

Wonsan is a port city located along the Sea of Japan. Smaller than Hamhung and Nampo, this coastal city provides a nice reprieve for those looking for tranquility.

Kim Jong-un has announced plans for over 600 million dollars in tourist development, with a new airport, golf courses, and world class hotels on the horizon

PLACES TO SEE

Changdokdo Lighthouse

For spectacular photos, take a sunset walk to the majestic Changdokdo Lighthouse, which is located on a tiny island reachable only via a narrow pedestrian bridge.

Take care of your electronics and try not to get washed away by one of the massive waves that frequently crash over the bridge.

Wonsan Revolutionary Train Museum

Originally opened in 1914, this station turned museum was the historic departing point for Kim Il-sung's journey to Pyongyang in 1945. Today, the train car as well as the wooden benches he sat on are on display.

Masik Ski Resort

Masik Ski Resort is only a 20-minute drive from Wonsan. Opened in 2013, this modern winter wonderland boasts modern facilities and a variety of slopes for all skill levels. If Kim Jong-un ever gets his wish of hosting a Winter

Olympics event in the Hermit Kingdom, you can be sure this will be where most of the events take place.

Songdowon International Children's Camp

Located on Songdowon Beach just outside of Wonsan, this summer camp is popular with locals and foreigners alike. Children from as far away as Tanzania, Mongolia, and Ireland travel to spend a one- or two-week session learning about North Korean ideology and interacting with local children.

Of course, this camp isn't only for propaganda. Water slides, video games, sports, and beach-swimming help fill out the action-packed days.

Man Gyong Bong 92 Ferry Ship

The out-of-commission Man Gyong 92 ferry ship used to transport up to 200 passengers from on the 28-hour trip form Wonsan to Niigata, Japan, where there is a strong North Korean population. Due to recent missile tests and increased tensions between the two countries, this ship has not made a commercial trip in over 13 years. Nonetheless, the ship was used to transport North Korean delegates to the 2018 Winter Olympics in South Korea.

PLACES TO EAT AND DRINK

Wonsan Seafood Restaurant

If you're a seafood lover, you really can't go wrong in Wonsan. Fresh caught fish is available everywhere, but my favorite place to eat is Wonsan Seafood Restaurant. Their plate of fried fish and chips offer a mouthwatering break from traditional Korean dishes. Other options include seafood barbeque, hairy crab, and sashimi.

PLACES TO SLEEP

Dongmyong Hotel

One of the more modern hotels in North Korea, the Dongmyong Hotel features picturesque views of Changdokdo Lighthouse and the Sea of Japan. The sounds of noisy fisherman may wake you up in the morning, helping you to get out of bed and enjoy all the nearby attractions in this centrally located hotel. Don't miss out on the hotel restaurant's delicious seafood, and also be sure to try your luck at the ping pong tables on the fourth floor.

CHAPTER 8

NATURE

Thanks to a lack of urban development, North Korea is one of the most rugged, unspoiled countries in the entire Asian continent.

Climate

North Korea has a humid continental climate, with warm balmy summers and cold dry winters. The rainiest time of year is July, where on average it rains 19 days. The rainy season is called "Changma". If you're chasing snow, December and January are ideal. May and September, to me, are the best times to visit, as the days are long, the temperatures typically hover around 64 degrees Fahrenheit, and there is minimal rainfall.

Kimjongilia And Kimilsungia: North Korean Flowers

The two deceased Kims join icons such as Princess Diana, Freddie Mercury, Michelle Obama, and Wolfgang Amadeus Mozart in having flowers named after them.

Kimilsungia is a violet colored hybrid orchid engineered in Indonesia by botanist Carl Bundt. Bundt named the flower after his daughter, Clara. However, after a visit by Kim Il-sung to Indonesia in 1965, then-Indonesian President Suharto renamed the flower Kimilsungia. While everyone in North Korea knows this beautiful flower as Kimilsungia, it is important to note the scientific name, recognized by the international community, is still Dendrobium Clara Bundt.

Kimjongilia was first cultivated by prolific Japanese botanist Kamo Mototeru. He presented it in 1988 to Jong-il as a token of friendship between Japan and Korea. Amazingly, this flower is designed to bloom every February 16, the day Jong-il was born. Red in color, it is a hybrid of an orchid and a begonia.

Animals of North Korea

While the DMZ may be a haven for endangered species, the rest of North Korea provides plenty of designated reserves for wildlife to thrive.

The Mongolian Wolf, Racoon Dogs (more foxlike than racoon-like), Eurasian Lynx, Asian Black Bears, Amur Hedgehogs, and the elk-like Manchurian Wapiti can all be found in North Korea.

The Pungsan species of dog, on display in the Pyongyang Zoo, is the National Dog of Korea. Appearance wise, this hunting dog looks like a cross between a German Shephard and the Japanese Shiba Inu. Several times in recent history, Pungsan dogs have been gifted from the leaders of North Korea to the leaders of South Korea as a sign of goodwill.

The Siberian Tiger is the National Animal of both Koreas, but sadly poaching has pushed them to the brink of extinction. I am not sure whether you would be lucky or unlucky to run into one. These elusive tigers continue to be spotted by farmers, hikers, and soldiers, particularly in and around the DMZ.

Aviphiles can find a rich assortment of 318 species of birds in North Korea. Due to increased industrialization in South Korea and China, birds have found sanctuary in the desolate countryside of North Korea. The highly territorial Northern Goshawk is the National Bird of North Korea. These birds rip through the skies tearing apart all sorts of prey, including rabbits, pigeons, pheasants, and anything else they can get their sharp claws on.

CHAPTER 9

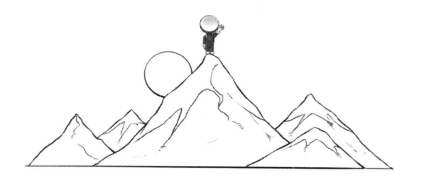

THE FIVE SACRED MOUNTAINS

There are five sacred mountains to the people of North Korea, each with their own unique folklore and geology. A visit to North Korea isn't complete without paying a visit to at least one of them.

1) Mount Chilbo

Chilbo is the most serene and least visited of the five mountains, and a great place to relax and enjoy the peace and quiet. It is known as the "Mountain of Seven Treasures" because, according to legend, there are seven treasures buried beneath this awe-inspiring mountain range. The Kaesim Buddhist Temple, which dates back to 826 AD, is considered a national treasure. If the season is right, you can harvest chestnuts from 200-year-old trees.

2) Mount Kumgang

"Diamond Mountain", as it is known to Koreans, is more beautiful than any gemstone I have encountered. Its stunning natural beauty and peaceful meadows are reminiscent of California's Yosemite National Park. Kumgang National Park stands just north of the border to South Korea.

For bird lovers, this is a great place to observe the endangered Red-Crowned Crane. A boat trip around Samil Lagoon and its tiny islands is a must on a warm summer day. Kuryong Falls, 243 feet tall and 13 feet wide, is a wonderous place to observe the raw power of nature.

For those seeking a spiritual experience, Kumgang has plenty of venues to help you achieve enlightenment. Pyohon Temple, which was founded in 670 AD, is one of the most heavenly Zen-Buddhist monasteries in all of Korea. In addition, the Podong Hermitage, dating back to 1676, features a small temple that dangles from a 60-foot cliff, reminiscent of the Tiger's Nest in Bhutan.

Joint Korean Tourist Zone

From 1998-2008, it was actually possible for South Koreans to visit Kumgang National Park. Hyundai, a South Korean automobile manufacturer, developed a resort in the region, and over one million South Korean citizens vacationed there.

On the morning of July 11, 2008, this partnership between the two Koreas came to a bloody end. A 53-year-old South Korean woman named Park Wang-ja was on her way to the beach when she entered an off-limits North Korean military zone and was shot to death by guards. When South Korea demanded a formal investigation, North Korea refused, and tours from the South have ceased.

Since then, tensions in this area have thawed a bit. In recent years, Kumgang has been chosen as a place for families separated by the Korean War to come and reunite.

3) Mount Kuwol

At only 3,130 feet tall, Kuwol is the smallest of the five Mountains. It is nicknamed the "September Mountain" because of its exceptional beauty during that month of the year. For history buffs, Kuwol was a major battle site during the Korean War. With its expansive forests it was a perfect hiding spot for North Korean guerilla fighters.

4) Mount Myohyang

The "Mysterious Fragrance" mountain certainly lives up to its name. Legend has it that Myohyang was the home of King Tangun, the first King of Korea, who descended from the heavens to the 3,310-foot summit over 4,000 years ago. Today it is home to beautiful hiking trails, wonderous animals like the Siberian Flying Squirrel, and the world-famous International Friendship Hall.

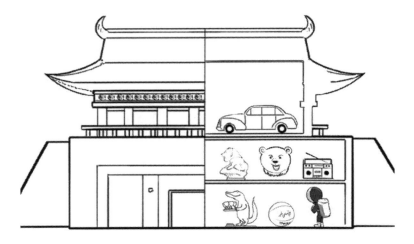

International Friendship Hall

Nestled in the peaceful surroundings of Mount Myohang sits the International Friendship Hall. Part museum, part time capsule, this building, which opened in 1978, houses a stunning collection of gifts to former leaders Kim Il-sung and Kim Jong-il. Many of the gifts were given by leaders and dignitaries of like-minded communist countries, such as a crocodile-skin suitcase from Cuba's Fidel Castro and a bulletproof limousine from the Soviet Union's Joseph Stalin. A signed basketball from Michael Jordan, Kim Jong-il's favorite basketball player, was gifted by then United States Secretary of State Madeline Albright in 2000.

5) Mount Paektu

Mount Paektu is an active volcano that last erupted in 1910. At 9,003 feet, it is the tallest mountain in the Korean Peninsula, and straddles the border with China. While it's theoretically possible to drive there, foreigners on group tours can only arrive via a small jet. The trip from Pyongyang to Samjiyon Airport, at the foot of Paektu, lasts an hour and a half. Due to harsh winter weather, the summit is only accessible from May to September.

Mount Paektu is most famous for being the alleged birthplace of Kim Jong-il. It is essentially a required stop when taking a trip to the mountain to visit the no-thrills log cabin where legend says the second Kim was born. His childhood toys, tools, binoculars, blankets, and other mementos are all proudly displayed.

Reaching the summit is a brisk, 40-minute climb from the bus parking lot. From the summit, it's about a five-minute walk down to the crater.

You can also visit Mount Paektu without going to North Korea, as it is accessible from the Chinese side.

Lake Tianchi

Also known as Heaven Lake, Lake Tianchi sits in the crater of Mount Paektu. It formed over 1,000 years ago in an eruption and is more than 1,100 feet deep. Legend has it that there are lake monsters that live here. According to various accounts, the Lake Tianchi Monsters are said to have seal-like bodies, five-foot-long necks, and human-like heads. The legend has become so famous that in 2008 an American band named The Mountain Goats released a song called *Lake Tianchi Monsters*.

Mount Paektu Vicinity

Samjiyon isn't only home to an airport, it's also a picturesque mountain village, complete with world class ski resorts in the winter and serene, refreshing alpine lakes in the summer.

Rimyongsu is a small village and home to the breathtaking Rimyongsu Falls. This multilayered rocky waterfall is beautifully capped by a traditional Korean pavilion. In the winter, the falls still flow, as the thermal water never freezes, thus creating a breathtaking snow-covered phenomenon.

CHAPTER 10

BOOKS

One of the best ways to travel is through your imagination, and there is no better tool to mobilize your imagination than a good book. Fortunately, in addition to my guide, there are stacks of books on North Korea that could keep you busy for years. Here are some of my favorites.

On the Juche Idea
Written by Kim Jong-il (1982)

This manifesto summarizes the self-sacrifice that the North Korean regime expects from their people. The book elaborates on Jong-il's father's description of the Juche philosophy, as well as emphasizing a Songun, or military first form of government.

With the Century
Written by Kim Il-sung (1992)

With almost 3,500 pages and covering only up to age 33, this eight-volume saga is perfect for those interested in the early years of the original Kim. While this book is required reading for every student in North Korea, it's banned in South Korea.

The Aquariums of Pyongyang: Ten Years in the North Korean Gulag
Written by Chol-hwan Kang (2005)

The author spent his youth, from age nine to 19, at Yodok, a North Korean prison camp. His heart-wrenching story chronicles life before, during, and after prison.

Pyongyang: A Journey in North Korea
Written by Guy Delisle (2007)

Pyongyang is a comical and informative graphic novel from the perspective of a lighthearted, mid 30's French-Canadian cartoonist. This novel was actually in the process of being made into a film starring Steve Carell, however, plans were scrapped following the controversy of the 2014 film, *The Interview.*

My Holiday in North Korea: Best/Worst Place on Earth
Written by Wendy Simmons (2016)

Simmons, a middle-aged American woman, chronicles her guided trip to North Korea through fascinating photos and humorous stories, drawing comparisons to *Alice in Wonderland* along the way.

The Girl with Seven Names
Written by Hyeonseo Lee (2016)

Famous for her TED talk, Lee grew up on the North Korean side of the Chinese border, and shares stories of not only her escape, but of life on the border, life as a refugee in China, and adapting to life in South Korea.

Not Forgotten: The True Story of My Imprisonment in North Korea
Written by Kenneth Bae and Mark Tabb (2016)

Not Forgotten is a first-hand account of the imprisonment of Kenneth Bae, a South Korean raised in the United States. After years of guiding tours to North Korea, he found himself apprehended after authorities found incriminating documents on his computer. His memoir does a great job showing the ups and downs of detainment in North Korea.

The Accusation: Forbidden Stories from Inside North Korea
Written by Bandi (2017)

Bandi is an anonymous North Korean writer who still lives in the Hermit Kingdom. This collection of short stories was smuggled out of North Korea by a defector and published once the manuscript made its way to South Korea. Today, these extraordinary tales of life within the Hermit Kingdom have been translated into over 20 languages.

Made in North Korea: Graphics from Everyday Life in the DPRK
Witten by Nick Bonner (2017)

This coffee table style book is perfect for students and admirers of communist design. Bonner, the founder of Koryo Tours, spent years photographing everything from comic books to canned foods, and compiles all these items into a visual history of North Korean design.

See You Again in Pyongyang
Written by Travis Jeppesen (2018)

This book is a travelogue of a college student studying abroad in Pyongyang for a month. His travels to some of the less famous tourist sites as well as his interactions with the local people are quite compelling.

CHAPTER 11

FILMS

Vladimir Lenin, one of the founding fathers of communism and a huge inspiration to the Juche Philosophy, once said that "Cinema is the most important of all arts." Movies are a big deal in North Korea and an integral cog in the propaganda machine. Unlike much of the rest of the world, nearly all films made in North Korea are produced by the government itself. Accordingly, most revolve around the Juche philosophy and war.

FEATURE FILMS MADE IN NORTH KOREA

My Home Village
Directed by Kang Hong-sik (1949)

As the first feature film made in North Korea, it is fitting that the plot involves the country's fight for independence from Japan. The story revolves around a peasant farmer who, after being imprisoned, joins up with resistance fighters and helps overthrow the Japanese occupation.

The Flower Girl
Directed by Choe Ik-gyu (1972)

The Flower Girl is the most iconic film North Korea has ever produced. So much so that the star of the film, Hong Yong-hee, appears on the one won banknote. The script was originally written by none other than Kim Il-sung as an opera in the 1930's, when it was a popular stage performance.

Salt
Directed by Shin Sang-ok (1985)

Salt changed the way films are made in North Korea. Its plot surrounding a Korean family torn apart by the Japanese occupation during the 1930s is a common theme in many

Korean films. However, the unique style, mature scenes, and hyper-realistic acting separate it from the typical campiness of earlier North Korean cinema. The lead actress of the film, Choi Eun-hee, won the Best Actress Award at the 1985 Moscow Film Festival.

Pulgasari
Directed by Shin Sang-ok (1985)

North Korea's answer to *Godzilla*, this bizarre monster flick was produced by Kim Jong-il with help from *Godzilla* producer Toho Cinemas. While Godzilla was a metaphor for the destructive atomic bomb in Japan, many believe Pulgasari is a symbol of the Soviet Union, which helped keep North Korea safe and established a strong protectorate of their way of life.

The film starts with a starving, imprisoned blacksmith, who makes a tiny doll named Pulgasari. When a drop of blood from the blacksmith's daughter falls on the doll, it comes to life. Pulgasari starts to eat iron, grows to the size of a human, and proceeds to help the villagers fight off the oppressive king. Sadly, Pulgasari can't stop growing, thanks to his healthy appetite for iron. Soon he goes from benevolent to a destructive force. Havoc ensues in this exciting thriller.

Comrade Kim Goes Flying
Directed by Kim Gwang-hun, Nicholas Bonner, and Anja Daelemans (2012)

This lighthearted romantic comedy is a throwback to films of the golden age of cinema. This historic film was made entirely in North Korea, with an all Korean cast, but financed with help from Belgian and English producers.

The story revolves around a young female coal miner who dreams of being a trapeze artist. It was screened at major film festivals around the world, including the Toronto and South Korean Film Festivals.

FEATURE FILMS ABOUT NORTH KOREA

North Korean Guys (South Korea)
Directed by Ahn Jin-woo (2003)

This light-hearted comedy follows two North Korean sailors who become shipwrecked in South Korea and have to find their way back home.

The Interview (USA)
Directed by Seth Rogan and Evan Goldberg (2014)

This may very well be the most controversial film in cinematic history. The plot, surrounding a fictional plan to assassinate Kim Jong-un, was perceived as a threat to North

Korean officials. The website of Sony Pictures, the film's distributor, was hacked in one of the most prolific cyber-attacks of all time.

Additionally, terrorist organizations threatened to attack any cinema that showed the film. As a result, the film only made 12 million dollars in box offices worldwide, a major disappointment for Sony Pictures.

The following movies are not necessarily focused on North Korea, buy they do have scenes set there:

- *Retreat, Hell! (1952)*

- *Spawn (1997)*

- *Die Another Day (2002)*

- *Team America: World Police (2004)*

- *Behind Enemy Lines 2: Axis of Evil (2006)*

- *Salt (2010)*

- *Red Dawn (2012)*

- *Olympus Has Fallen (2013)*

DOCUMENTARIES

Defilada
Directed by Andrzej Fidyk (1988)

One of the first documentaries to expose the North Korean regime, *Defilada* (meaning "The Parade" in Polish) is the work of Polish director Andrzej Fidyk. Despite its critique of the totalitarian government then run by Kim Il-sung, North Korea praised its truthful depiction.

Game of Their Lives
Directed by Daniel Gordon (2002)

This exciting documentary tells the story of the North Korean national men's soccer team's unlikely rise to the quarterfinals of the 1966 FIFA World Cup.

A State of Mind
Directed by Nicholas Bonner (2004)

Providing a rare behind the scenes look at the Mass Games, this film follows two North Korean gymnasts and their vigorous training regimen leading up to the 2003 Games.

Dear Pyongyang
Directed by Yang Yong-hi (2005)

This beautiful selection of the Sundance Film Festival provides an incredibly intimate glimpse at children who were sent by their parents from Osaka, Japan to Pyongyang, North Korea to live and be educated under the communist regime.

Abduction: The Megumi Yokota Story
Directed by Patty Kim and Chris Sheridan (2006)

Winner at the Austin, Omaha, and Slamdance Film Festivals, this is the heartbreaking story of the kidnapping of a Japanese teenager by North Korean agents. You can read more about this in Chapter 17.

Crossing the Line
Directed by Daniel Gordon and Nicholas Bonner (2006)

American soldier Joe Dresnok crossed the Demilitarized Zone in August of 1962, and never looked back. This poignant documentary chronicles his now seemingly happy life in North Korea, where he is married and has even starred in popular North Korean films such as *Unsung Heroes*, where he plays the American villain. Narrated by

Golden Globe Award winning actor Christian Slater, this is my favorite of the documentaries on North Korea.

Yodok Stories
Directed by Andrzej Fidyk (2008)

Twenty years after *Defilada*, Fidyk returned to the subject of North Korea with his portrayal of Yodok Concentration Camp, one of the country's most notorious. Through the accounts of those who have survived and escaped Yodok, Fidyk paints a horrific picture of what life was like inside the now closed concentration camp.

Kimjongilia
Directed by N. C. Heiken (2008)

A 2009 selection of the Sundance Film Festival, *Kimjongilia* successfully demonstrates the brutality of the regime. Through several interviews, survivors speak of the inhumane conditions that forced them to risk their lives for freedom.

Dennis Rodman's Big Bang in Pyongyang
Directed by Colin Offland (2015)

This 2015 documentary chronicles Dennis Rodman's chaotic, controversial, and alcohol-fueled visit to Pyongyang with a team of fellow American basketball players. The trip was overshadowed by the American media's insistence that Rodman help release American prisoner Kenneth Bae, which results in many a confrontation with everyone from his NBA All-Star teammates to CNN Anchor Chris Cuomo.

I Am Sun-Mu
Directed by Adam Sjoberg (2015)

Sun Mu is without a doubt the most successful and proficient artist to come out of North Korea in recent memory.

Directed by Adam Sjoberg, this 2015 documentary follows Sun Mu during an exhibition he tries to put on in Beijing, China. Sun Mu never reveals his face to the public, as he escaped North Korea and his identity could put the lives of his family left behind in danger. His art is truly exceptional and puts a "pop art" twist on traditional North Korean scenes.

Secret State: Inside North Korea
Produced by CNN (2018)

In June 2018, CNN sent American journalist Will Ripley to explore North Korea. Ripley and his team spent 16 days exploring the Hermit Kingdom. Their stops included

Mount Paektu, the DMZ, local arcades, and even a smart phone shop. I truly enjoyed this unbiased look at life in North Korea, and I believe this approach is the reason Ripley is repeatedly allowed access into North Korea.

CHAPTER 12

MUSIC

While North Korea may still be heavily insulated, its music scene has become more and more diverse in recent years. From the traditional folk songs to the modern North "K-Pop" of today, music lovers can rejoice in the delightful tunes coming out of the Hermit Kingdom.

Traditional Music

Taejung Kayo is a patriotic style of music, in which a female singer is accompanied by a large orchestral ensemble. The music is similar to that of old Spaghetti Western movies, and the lyrics to the songs are meant to instill party loyalty in its listeners.

North Korean folk songs are extremely popular and heavily promoted by the government to strengthen national pride. The Juche philosophy applies to music in the sense that there are rarely ever solos. Most students learn at least one instrument as part of their curriculum in primary school, and students with exceptional talent are given additional lessons and sent to specialty music schools to further develop their skills.

Pochonbo Electronic Ensemble

If you visit Pyongyang, you are guaranteed to hear a song from this great artist. That's because every morning at 6:00 a.m., the same song blares from every loudspeaker for everyone in the city to hear. That song is Pochonbo's own *Where Are You, Dear General?*

The group was named after the 1937 Battle of Pochonbo, in which Kim Il-sung led guerrilla forces in an attack on Japanese occupying forces. Famous for more than just the "wake-up song", their unique 80's sound blends electric guitars and synthesizers with traditional Korean folk music. Their song, *Glad to Meet You*, about friendly relations with

South Korea, has become the official anthem of peace talks.

Moranbong

To compete with South Korea's massively popular "K-Pop" music genre, Kim Jong-un himself established an all-female North Korean pop band named Moranbong.

Dressed in high heels and mini-skirts, their performances involve epic electric guitar solos, violins, keyboards and pyrotechnics. Several performances are available for your viewing pleasure on YouTube. I would recommend the *North Korea Disney Show*, featuring costumed characters or a cover of Frank Sinatra's *My Way*, for travelers who like the oldies.

Hye-Yeong Jeon's "The Whistle Song"

This kid-friendly song by pop star Hye-yeong Jeon sounds like something out of *Snow White and the Seven Dwarfs*. Its super catchy chorus will get stuck in your head for days and is a shining example of the optimism displayed by the people of North Korea.

Laibach- The First Foreign Rock Band to Play North Korea

After North Korean officials saw the music video for the song *The Whistleblowers* by Slovenian industrial rock band Laibach, they were driven to invite the band to perform in Pyongyang. In August 2015, Laibach became the first rock band to play North Korea, commemorating the 70th anniversary of the end of Japanese occupation. In addition to their own original songs, they played music from *The Sound of Music* and The Beatles' *Across the Universe*, as well as a rendition of the unofficial North Korean anthem, *Arirang*. For more on this epic event, watch the BBC produced documentary *When Rock Arrived in North Korea: Liberation Day*.

Damon Albarn Visits

Damon Albarn, the front man of massively popular British rock band Blur, visited Pyongyang in 2013. His visit inspired the bands haunting song *Pyongyang*, featured on their 2015 album *The Magic Whip*. He told British newspaper The Sun, "It's about the day I spent visiting the mausoleum of the Great Leaders and the trees were talking to me, that's what I call propaganda!"

Albarn, also the front man of the Gorillaz, used Pyongyang again as a subject for the band's 2017 music video for their song, *Sleeping Powder*. In the video, Albarn's avatar dances around a backdrop of the Mass Games and Pyongyang Circus.

Spring is Coming Concert Series

During the 2018 Winter Olympics in South Korea, North Korea's Samjiyon Orchestra performed several concerts in front of South Korean President Moon Jae-in.

As an act of goodwill, in April of 2018 South Korea reciprocated. Approximately 200 South Korean delegates, musicians, journalists, and athletes arrived at the East Pyongyang Grand Theatre to perform in front of 1,500 lucky citizens, including Kim Jong-un.

The audience was treated to performances from a diverse array of artists, including South Korean rock band YB, the all-girl K-Pop band Red Velvet, and taekwondo performers.

Joss Stone Plays North Korea

Another British singer, Joss Stone, visited North Korea in March of 2019, as part of her five year "Total World Tour" quest to play every country in the world. Stone performed many of her own songs, as well as *Arirang*, in a local bar in front of a crowd comprised mainly of tourists.

CHAPTER 13

VIDEO GAMES

Perhaps the most fun way for travelers to familiarize themselves with North Korea is through video games. In these games, you are not being watched 24/7 by a government minder and you are allowed to roam the streets, countryside, and even the DMZ on your own. While household video game systems aren't readily available to North Koreans, arcades appear in many cities.

GAMES BY NORTH KOREANS

Pyongyang Racer (2012)

Created by students at Kim Chaek University of Technology, Korea's version of *Gran Turismo* features North Korean manufactured cars driving around the empty streets of Pyongyang. The famous traffic ladies help lead drivers in the right direction.

Hunting Yankee (2017)

This game, created by the North Korean Advanced Technology Research Institute, allows players to shoot American soldiers from behind enemy lines. The gameplay is similar to first person shooter games such as *Call of Duty.*

GAMES ABOUT NORTH KOREA

Tom Clancy's Ghost Recon 2 (2004)

This massively popular sequel takes place entirely on the Korean peninsula. Play as a Ghost, a special American combat unit similar to the Navy Seals. The storyline involves the fictional General Jung Soon, a North Korean commander similar to Kim Jong-il. When Soon threatens to start a new Korean War, you must battle the North Koreans, crossing the DMZ, blowing up military bases, and destroying nuclear warheads.

Mercenaries: Playground of Destruction (2005)

Mercenaries allows players to take part in a new Korean War. In the game, fictional North Korean President Choi Kim announces that North Korea will peacefully reunify with South Korea. Unexpectedly, a military coup takes place and North Korea is taken over with a new, even more evil regime. With the country in absolute chaos, forces from China and Russia fight for control, along with American and South Korean soldiers. Produced by LucasArts, a fun feature of this game is the ability to play as popular film characters Indiana Jones and Han Solo.

Rogue Warrior (2009)

While *Rogue Warrior* is infamous for being one of the worst games of all time, it's the only game in which players travel back in time to 1986 to visit Unggi, which is located within the Rason Special Economic Zone. Here, players are sent to gather intel on ballistic missiles.

CHAPTER 14

SPORTS

The United States' influence in South Korea helped baseball become massively popular. In fact, over 20 South Koreans have gone on to play Major League Baseball. In contrast, baseball is rarely played in North Korea. It is certainly clear that the Soviet/Chinese influence has not only influenced politics, but sports too.

The World Cup

Soccer and basketball are by far the most popular team sports in the Hermit Kingdom. North Korea's men's soccer team was admitted into FIFA in 1958 and competed in their first World Cup in 1966. After defeating Italy in stunning fashion, North Korea lost to Portugal in the quarter-finals. Their first World Cup was their most successful, and they wouldn't compete again until 2010, when they were winless and eliminated in group play.

The North Korean women's soccer team qualified for four straight World Cup tournaments, reaching the quarterfinals in 2007. In 2015, the team was banned amidst a doping scandal, and they have not played in a World Cup since.

Pyongyang Marathon

If you are looking to compete against North Koreans themselves, look no further than the Pyongyang Marathon, which takes place every April. The race starts and ends at May Day Stadium in Pyongyang, and it also features half-marathon, along with five and ten kilometer races.

Olympics

North Korea first competed in the Olympics in 1964, and they have since earned 56 medals. They have had most of their Olympic success in weightlifting, earning 16 medals in this sport alone, five of them gold.

The 2018 Winter Olympics, held in PyeongChang, South Korea, were quite significant. North and South Korea joined forces on the Olympic stage in the women's ice hockey event, forming one team. While unsuccessful in their chase for a medal, it was a symbolic win for the future of the Korean peninsula.

The Korean Reunification Flag

The Korean Reunification Flag, also known as the Blue Flag, is a symbolic flag used mainly at sporting events. Depicting a blue Korea with a white background, this flag presents Korea as one, without borders.

The flag was first introduced at the 1990 Asian Games in Beijing, China, where North and South Korea first competed as a single team. It was again used at the 1991 World Table Tennis Championship in Chiba, Japan, where the unified Korean women's team won a gold medal.

Since then, the flag has been carried symbolically at various sporting events, including the opening ceremonies of the 2000, 2004, 2006, and 2018 Olympics.

Professional Wrestling

In 1995, superstars from World Championship Wrestling (WCW) and New Japan Pro Wrestling (NJPW) combined to host the Collision in Korea Pay-Per-View event. This two-day event took place at May Day Stadium in Pyongyang and was attended by an estimated 320,000 people. The main event featured Japanese wrestling legend Antonio Inoki defeating the "Nature Boy", Ric Flair.

May Day Stadium

Opened on May 1, 1989, May Day Stadium is the largest sporting venue in the world. With a capacity of over 114,000 spectators, this gargantuan stadium has hosted everything from the Mass Games to speeches by former United States

Secretary of State Madeline Albright and current South Korean President Moon Jae-in.

Dennis and Kim

Perhaps one of the strangest friendships in the world is between basketball Hall of Famer Dennis "The Worm" Rodman and Kim Jong-un. In 2013, North Korea requested Chicago Bulls legend Michael Jordan to visit the Hermit Kingdom at the request of Jong-un. Jordan declined and Jong-un then reached out to his second favorite player, Dennis Rodman, who accepted.

Rodman has won five NBA championships and is widely considered the greatest rebounder of all time, but is perhaps more well known for his off the court antics. He has starred in movies alongside action hero Jean Claude Van Dam, appeared in professional wrestling matches alongside Hulk Hogan, dated pop star Madonna, and wore a wedding dress while marrying television star Carmen Electra.

Over the years, Rodman has visited North Korea several times, bringing former players to compete in exhibitions in front of Kim and thousands of citizens.

CHAPTER 15

HOLIDAYS AND EVENTS

HOLIDAYS

January 1	New Year's Day
February 16	Kim Jong-il's Birthday
April 25	Kim Il-sung's Birthday Korean People's Army Day
July 8	Anniversary of Kim Il-sung's Death
July 27	Korean War Victory Day
August 15	National Liberation Day
September 9	Day of the Foundation of the DPRK, (typical start date of the Mass Games)
October 10	Day of the Foundation of the Workers Party of the DPRK
December 27	Day of the Promulgation of Socialist Constitution of DPRK
December 31	New Year's Eve

In addition to these National Holidays, North Korean observe dozens of days on the calendar in honor of farmers, fishermen, geological surveyors, miners, children, and other members of Korean society. Chuseok, which is the Korean Thanksgiving, takes place in September or October, depending on the lunar calendar.

Mass Games

The tradition of mass games goes back to Germany during the 1800s, where soldiers trained in unison. It evolved throughout the next century to the point where it became performance art in the Soviet Union. Socialist countries like

East Germany, Bulgaria, and Romania all had different variations of the Mass Games.

Kim Il-sung was inspired to hold the first games in 1961, telling the people of North Korea that "Developing mass gymnastics is important in training children to be a fully developed communist man." In 1983, Il-sung would open up a special school devoted to children who would one day perform in the Mass Games.

The Mass Games were held every year from 2002-2013 (except 2006), and after a five-year hiatus returned in 2018. Today, over 100,000 North Koreans perform in the Mass Games every summer. Performers as young as five years old dance, sing, perform acrobatic tricks, and hold up colored placards, creating what can only be described as a human LED screen. Performances last approximately 90 minutes.

There is nothing in the world like the Mass Games. It is more magical than the Northern Lights and more entertaining than any Super Bowl Halftime Show or Olympic Opening Ceremony. If you get the opportunity to include it on your trip, jump on it. If not, sit down with a bowl of microwave popcorn and watch one of the many recordings available on YouTube.

CHAPTER 16

FOOD AND DRINK

Visit South Korea and you will be able to grab breakfast at Dunkin Donuts or dinner at the Hard Rock Café. In North Korea, you won't find any worldwide food chains. Embrace this opportunity and be sure to sample several of the delicacies I have recommended here for you.

WHAT TO EAT

Air Koryo Burger

Better pack a snack for your flight as this may be the worst burger you'll ever eat. Taking the stereotype of bad airplane food to a whole other level, this "burger" is served cold, the meat is cream colored, the bread is often stale, and it is topped off with a slice of cheese and a sprinkle of purple cabbage. On the plus side, it's free (with the purchase of a plane ticket), and there is a vegetarian option available (bread, cheese, and cabbage).

Bulgogi

Korean barbeque is famous the world-over. If you are looking for an authentic North Korean take on this increasingly popular fad, look no further than bulgogi. Small table-top stoves are brought to the dinner table, where you and your companions can marinate various meats in garlic, onions or whatever other delicious condiments are provided. Nothing is as fresh as a meal cooked at your table!

Gangjeong

These deep-fried honey infused rice puffs provide a fun snack for long bus rides or hiking trips. They are also usually served at weddings and other celebrations and are available in a variety of flavors such as peanut, sesame, and cinnamon.

Gyeran-Mari

This is North Korea's version of the popular Asian-American fast food egg roll. Small pieces of rolled up egg omelet are filled with either veggies, meats, seafood, or cheese. This light snack is the perfect appetizer to a big meal.

Haejang-guk

"Hangover soup", as the locals refer to it, is popular after a night out or on a cold winter day. Like other Korean dishes, this brothy soup can be comprised of various ingredients, however, dried cabbage, veggies, and beef are the best-known types. For adventurous foodies, ask for seonji-guk, which is made with coagulated ox blood.

Jeon

Coated in flour and egg and then pan fried, jeon is not exactly what you would call a healthy food. Nevertheless, they are one of the most delicious snacks in the entire world. Similar in taste and texture to the eastern European "latke", jeon have been a staple in the Korean diet since the first kings took over the peninsula. Fillings vary and include meat, poultry, vegetable, and seafood. Virtually anything edible can be put inside these tasty "Korean pancakes". For a sweet romantic desert, try the jangmi-hwajeon, made of edible roses.

Kimchi

Kimchi is one of the most internationally popular dishes in both North and South Korea. Made out of a base of cabbage, kimchi pairs great with any dish. There are several ways to prepare it, and it tastes fantastic whether eaten salty, spicy, or as a soup. It is also an important way for citizens in the rural countryside to get their vitamins in the winter, as kimchi is packed with Vitamins A and C, as well as fiber.

Neng Myon

Neng myon is a bowl of delicious, refreshing, ice-cold buckwheat noodles, typically prepared with meat, egg, and an assortment of sauces. The best in the country is found in Pyongyang.

Petrol Clams

These are clams cooked with gasoline. Participating in this fun tradition, particularly on a cold night, is a fun way to both snack on fresh seafood and interact with fellow North Koreans and travelers. Sit by the fire while your bus driver pours gasoline on the clams. Yes, they taste a bit…gassy, and yes, eat at your own risk.

"Sweet Meat"

Citizens from Korea, both North and South, as well as countries like China and the Philippines, partake in an activity much of the rest of the Western world could never even fathom; they eat dog. If you are offered sweet meat in North Korea, be well aware that this is our canine friend.

Sweet meat often comes in the form of boshitang, or dog meat soup, consisting of cooked dog, onions, dandelions, and spices. The best place for tourists to try this dish is at Tongil Restaurant in Kaesong City.

While I would never eat dog based on my friendly encounters with this loving, loyal creature of Earth, it is important not to judge the North Koreans for doing so. In India, many find it appalling to eat cow. In Israel, most locals frown upon eating pig. Different countries have different views on what is and what is not okay to eat, and it's important for us travelers to be keep an open mind about this.

Taedonggang Sungeo-guk

While New England has its clam chowder, Pyongyang is famous for its grey mullet fish soup straight from the Taedong River. Complimented with red paste, peppers, and garlic, this spicy soup will leave you asking for seconds.

Wild Pine Mushrooms

Known for their distinct flavor and pleasant scent, wild pine mushrooms grow in abundance in North Korea. In fact, they are so popular, Kim Jong-un sent two tons of them (estimated value of 2.6 million dollars) to South Korean President Moon Jae-in as part of the 2018 Peace Summit.

WHAT TO DRINK

Ginseng Tea

This delicious traditional tea is a one stop medicinal shop. Ginseng has been proven to enhance memory, boost your immune system, increase energy levels, lower blood sugar, reduce inflammation, and may help fight cancer. While ginseng is enjoyed worldwide, many enthusiasts say that the best can be find in Kaesong City, North Korea.

Jujube Tea

This nutritious maroon colored tea is said to help lessen stress among those who consume it. Made of the jujube fruit (a type of date), it is typically brewed over a span of eight hours and usually served with a topping of fresh pine nuts.

Nongtaegi

Also known as soju, it is a clear alcohol comprised of barley or potato extract. Fans of the Japanese spirit, sake, will find the taste and effects of nongtaegi to be very similar.

Taedonggang Beer

Taedonggang beer was founded by the North Korean government in 2002. After importing brewing equipment from a nineteenth century brewery in Wiltshire, England, the Taedonggang Brewery was up and running. This five-percent alcohol lager is a little on the bitter side but enjoyed by Koreans and foreigners alike.

CHAPTER 17

HUMAN RIGHTS

Sadly, there is a dark side to this country of hospitable people, delicious food, and glorious nature. All the goodness is overshadowed by the fact that each year countless citizens risk their lives to escape, and countless others die in many of the countries infamous prison camps.

Prison Camps

Much of North Korea's atrocious human rights records are centered around its prison system. While exact facts and figures are not made public by the North Korean government, defectors have described horrible conditions not seen since the Holocaust.

Many prisons are filled with political prisoners. Speaking out against the government, plotting an escape, and not respecting the leaders or their philosophy are all common reasons for citizens to be imprisoned. One defector claims that a prisoner was sentenced to years in jail for being caught singing a South Korean pop song.

In North Korea, you can also be imprisoned for crimes your relatives commit. For instance, defectors claim that their families were imprisoned as punishment for their escape. If a prisoner is or gets pregnant, her baby will be born in prison, assuming the prisoner is fortunate enough to get sufficient nourishment to sustain the pregnancy.

According to human rights specialists, there are approximately 100,000 prisoners in North Korea today. It is further estimated that anywhere from 20 to 40 percent of these prisoners die from malnutrition or starvation.

Lee Soon-ok, who defected to China, testified before the United States Congress and described horrid conditions including the use of water torture on prisoners. This form of torture has left her permanently disabled.

Other defectors have described, in detail, conditions of North Korea's two most infamous concentration camps, Yodok and Kaechon. At Yodok, which closed in 2014, survivors described 14 hour forced work shifts, followed by a measly dinner and a two-hour lesson on North Korean ideology. At Kaechon, former prisoners tell of sharing a cramped 322 square foot cell with 80 other prisoners. Typical meals consist of salt soup and corn, and when there are shortages, prisoners resort to eating anything they can find, even rats.

They say history repeats itself. The Holocaust concentration camps, the terror cells of Guantanamo, and the gulags of the former Soviet Union should serve as reminders that history does indeed repeat itself if people do not learn its valuable lessons.

Freedom of Press

Currently in the United States, there is a war with the press. For example, depending on the channel you turn to or newspaper you read, you will hear a different opinion of current United States President Donald Trump. In North Korea, there is only one acceptable opinion.

The media of North Korea is completely controlled by the government. No matter which newspaper you read, you will be fed stories about how great Kim Jong-un is, and how evil their political adversaries like Japan and the United States are.

Outside of the political elite, access to the internet is virtually inaccessible. For those who can log on in institutions like the Pyongyang Library, they will find their search results to be severely filtered and monitored by the government.

If any staff member of the press were to attempt to write a critique of their own government, the punishment would surely be imprisonment, if not death.

Freedom of Religion

Like China, Vietnam, and the former Soviet Union, North Korea is officially an atheist state. Western religion of any kind (Christianity, Judaism, Islam, etc.) is simply not tolerated for any citizen of North Korea.

It should be noted that it has not always been this way. Prior to the 1890's and the Japanese Occupation of the Korean peninsula, Pyongyang was known as the "Jerusalem of the East", with its large Christian population.

While it is true that there are several churches in and around Pyongyang today, these only open to foreigners, particularly those who are living and working in Pyongyang.

For North Koreans, being in possession of any type of religious symbol or text is highly dangerous, and there have been unverified reports that those caught are subject to death. Kim Il-sung, Kim Jong-il, and Kim Jong-un are the closest thing the Korean people have to God. If they don't believe in and respect them, they will be severely punished.

Billy Graham's Visit

By this point in my guide, you should know that sometimes North Korea defies practical logic. Believe it or not, Billy Graham, "America's Pastor", visited North Korea not once, but twice.

In 1992, Graham visited Pyongyang, giving lectures and even having private meetings with Kim Il-sung. His goal was to establish a relationship in the Hermit Kingdom, where maybe one day he could spread the word of God.

In 1994, Graham visited again, this time to ease tensions after the first wave of North Korean nuclear tests.

While his vision of introducing Evangelical Christianity to North Korea didn't turn out as planned, Evangelicals today are one of the few organizations allowed to give humanitarian aid to the people of North Korea.

Freedom of Travel

For North Korean citizens, not only is it nearly impossible to leave the country, but it's also extremely difficult to leave your own city. Travel for the sake of traveling is not possible without government permission.

The very few lucky ones who are allowed to leave the

country are typically either political elites or athletes competing in international competition. If you are fortunate enough to be in one of these groups, escaping and seeking asylum is extremely complicated. For one, government caretakers will be watching your every move, and if you do manage to escape, your relatives back home will surely be punished for your actions.

For ordinary citizens trying to escape, whether through China in the north or South Korea in the south, punishments range from years of forced labor to death.

Kidnappings and Abductions

North Korea has a long and troubled history of kidnappings. South Korea and Japan, two of North Korea's closest neighbors, have been impacted the most by these heinous crimes.

South Korean Kidnappings

During the Korean War, it was reported that over 80,000 South Korean citizens were abducted and brought over to the North. The goal of these abductions was to strip South Korea of some of their brightest citizens and use them to build up North Korea. Doctors, teachers, politicians, and successful businessmen were among those targeted as victims.

Kidnappings didn't cease following the armistice agreement ending the Korean War. While kidnapping citizens from South Korea in their native country has become increasingly rare in recent years, kidnapping them from neutral or disputed territories has not.

In Norway, Macau, Singapore, and China there have been instances of North Korean authorities apprehending innocent South Koreans against their will. South Korean fishermen off the coast of South Korea have long been targets for North Korean officials. There are over 400 missing South Korean fishermen today, many believed to be detained in North Korea.

North Korea vehemently denies any involvement in the kidnappings of South Koreans after the armistice. They claim that all South Koreans in North Korea today chose to be there on their own.

Abduction of South Korean Movie Stars

During the early 1970's, Kim Jong-il was dissatisfied with his country's lackluster effect on international cinema. The thriving South Korean film industry didn't make matters any better.

Enter Choi Eun-hee, a beautiful and talented South Korean actress. In 1978, after having trouble finding work, she agreed to meet film producers in Hong Kong to discuss a new film project. Following their meeting, the producers decided to give her the role. Little did she know this role would be the first of many, all forced upon her by the North Korean government.

She was brought to Nampo Harbor, where she was imprisoned in a lavish villa and educated in the Juche Ideology.

Her ex-husband, famous South Korean director Shin Sang-ok, flew to Hong Kong where his wife had last been seen in an effort to find her. After failing in his search for her, he was also approached by "producers", taken to North Korea, and imprisoned when he tried to escape.

After years of being forced to watch four films a day, critique them, and have in-depth discussions with folks from the North Korean film industry (including Kim Il-sung and Kim Jong-il), Shin and Choi were reunited at a party in Pyongyang.

Shin would go on to make six films in North Korea, four of them starring Choi. With classics such as *Salt* and *Pulgasari*, North Korea finally was seen as a force in international cinema.

During a 1986 visit to Vienna to secure financing for a new film, Shin and Choi devised their escape plan. After convincing their North Korean bodyguards to leave them alone for an interview, the couple ran into a cab and demanded to be taken to the United States embassy. With their bodyguards chasing them through traffic, Shin and Choi were able to narrowly escape and reach the embassy safely.

The couple was granted asylum and eventually moved to Beverly Hills, California. Shin directed his final film, the 1995 cult classic *3 Ninjas Knuckle Up*, under the pseudonym Simon Sheen. Choi, after her traumatic experience in North Korea, would never act again.

Japanese Kidnappings

The Japanese government has reported 17 missing citizens over the years. In 2002, then-leader Kim Jong-il admitted to kidnapping 13 of these citizens. Jong-il apologized to the Japanese government for North Korea's involvement in the kidnappings and returned the five surviving hostages to Japan (the other eight were reported dead).

The Tragic Story of Megumi Yokota

On a cold autumn day in 1977 in a sleepy Japanese fishing village, a 13-year-old girl named Megumi Yokota walked home alone from school. That walk would be her last steps taken in her home country.

For years, her disappearance was a mystery. Almost 20 years after she vanished her parents were notified that Yokota was suspected to be in North Korea. In 2002, the North Korean government admitted to kidnapping Yokota.

Yokota was kidnapped by North Korean agents and forced onto a boat bound for North Korea. Once there, she was forced to learn Korean and train spies on how to act Japanese. Sadly, North Korean authorities claim she committed suicide in 1994. When her ashes were returned to her parents in Japan, DNA tests concluded that the ashes were not Yokota's. What really happened to Yokota remains a mystery to this day.

In Japan, she has become somewhat of a mythical figure. Many Japanese people believe she is still alive somewhere and will one day return home. Her story has inspired artists all over the world. *Megumi*, a 2004 manga (Japanese comic book) about her life before the abduction was turned into a popular anime series in Japan. The documentary, *The Abduction of Megumi Yokota*, was a critical and commercial success. In music, British pop star Peter Frampton wrote two songs dedicated to her, *Asleep at the Wheel*, and the haunting instrumental track *Suite Liberte*. Furthermore, Paul Stookey of the legendary folk band, Peter, Paul, and Mary, wrote *Song for Megumi* in her honor, and toured Japan playing it in front of emotional crowds.

Assassinations and Executions

As a means of keeping control of the regime, the North Korean government finds it necessary to remove those deemed enemies or threats. While most countries simply remove such officials from office or at worst imprison them,

North Korea chooses to kill them. Various news sources have reported hundreds of executions since Kim Jong-un's rise to power in 2011, but executions go back to the days of Kim Il-sung. The exact number of victims is unverifiable as North Korea rarely publicly announces them. Several incidents have been documented over the years, some of which are listed below.

Execution of Woo In-Hee

Woo In-hee was a famous actress widely considered to be the most beautiful woman on the Korean peninsula. Despite her being married to Yoo Hosun, one of the most prolific directors in North Korean history, she had a reputation for committing adulterous acts.

Sometimes her affairs led her to cameramen or production assistants, however, at some point in the late 1970's, she began an affair with none other than Kim Jong-il. Like her other flings, she could not stay faithful, and soon matched up with a young Korean-Japanese disc jockey.

Jong-il was furious when he found out that his mistress was seeing other people, and ruthlessly had her executed by firing squad in front of 6,000 people.

Her tragic death in 1981 not only ended her life, but also erased her from film history. Jong-il had her scenes removed from every film she ever appeared in.

Execution of So Kwan Hui

Accusations of being a spy for the United States and sabotaging the North Korean government during the mid-1990's led to an early death for the former Minister of Agriculture, So Kwan-hui. He was killed by firing squad in 1997.

Execution of Jang Song-Thaek

Jang Song-thaek, uncle of Kim Jong-un and vice-chairman of the National Defense Commission, was considered the second most powerful man in North Korea before his death. He was executed by firing squad on December 12, 2013, after being accused of being anti-party and counter revolutionary.

Execution of Kim Yong-Jin

The former Deputy Premier for Education was found to be in a "disrespectful posture" during a meeting and subsequently was killed by a firing squad in 2016.

Assassination of Kim Jong-Nam

Kim Jong-nam was the eldest son of Kim Jong-il, half-brother of Kim Jong-un, and long believed to be the successor to his father. Things seemed to be on track for Jong-nam until a failed visit (traveling on an invalid passport) to Tokyo Disneyland in 2001 brought embarrassment to the regime. His later attempts at government reform and his openness to capitalism exiled him from his father and ended any hope of him taking over as leader.

After his father's death in 2011, Jong-nam left North Korea. For years, he lived in hiding in Macau, rarely giving interviews or being spotted by the media. He feared for his life and wrote letters to his half-brother pleading to have mercy on him.

Unfortunately, things ended abruptly for Jong-nam in February of 2017. Two Vietnamese women walked up to him and rubbed a deadly chemical agent known as VX in his face at Kuala Lampur International Airport in Malaysia. He died within minutes at the age of 45.

The women claimed that they were told by Jong-nam's "friends" that it was a prank for a Korean television show, and they were given reduced sentences. The four North Koreans accused of masterminding the plot were cleared by Malaysian authorities and allowed to return to Pyongyang.

Acts of Terrorism

Acts of terrorism have plagued planet Earth for much of the past century. Terrorism attacks are different from war as they often target civilians, not soldiers. Additionally, rules don't seem to apply to terrorism.

Korean Airlines Hijacking

On a frigid winter's day in December of 1969, a Korean Airlines flight took off from Gangneung, South Korea destined for Seoul, South Korea. Instead, the plane landed in Wonsan, North Korea. Survivors claim that a passenger stepped into the cockpit and hijacked the plane. The North Korean government refutes this, saying the South Korean pilots chose to fly the plane to Wonsan and land there.

After months of negotiations, 39 of the passengers were released and walked across the Joint Security Area back to their homes in South Korea. However, seven of the passengers and four crew-members were never to be seen again.

The Bombing in Rangoon

On October 9, 1983, there was a failed assassination attempt on then South Korean President Chun Doo-hwan in Rangoon, Burma (present-day Yangon, Myanmar). While Doo-hwan escaped the bombing because he was stuck in traffic, 21 people were killed and 46 injured. Included in the casualties were many high ranking South Korean politicians who were on a diplomatic visit to Burma.

Following a manhunt, one suspect was killed in a shootout, and two others apprehended. After confessing, one surviving suspect received life in prison, the other less cooperative suspect was hung. To this day, the North Korean government denies any involvement in the attack.

The Bombing of Korean Air Flight 858

Korean Air Flight 858 departed Baghdad bound for Seoul on November 29, 1987, with scheduled stops in Abu Dhabi and Bangkok. After its first stop in Abu Dhabi, two North Koreans disembarked the plane. The remaining 115 passengers, 113 of which were South Korean, would meet their doom when a bomb exploded shortly after takeoff.

The North Koreans immediately tried to escape and get another plane out of Abu Dhabi, however, they were stopped and apprehended by local police. Kim Sung-il and his accomplice Kim Hyon-hui both took cyanide pills to try and kill themselves before answering any questions.

Miraculously, Hyon-hui survived her suicide attempt. The South Korean government sentenced her to death for her part in the murder. Shortly after her sentencing, then South Korean President Roh Tae-woo pardoned her, claiming that she was brainwashed by the North Korean government. Today, she lives in South Korea where she is an advocate for human rights and regularly gives interviews on relations between the two Koreas.

North Korea has denied involvement in this attack, claiming it was a conspiracy and that the two suspects were, in fact, South Koreans.

Foreigner Imprisonments

There have been 25 non-military foreigners who have been imprisoned in North Korea since 1996. One from Australia, one from Canada, five from South Korea, and eighteen from the United States.

When visiting North Korea, you must be cognizant of the strict laws that are enforced. Some of the things people do to get arrested in North Korea are not even crimes in the rest of the world. Many foreigners have been arrested for simply leaving a bible somewhere or speaking to locals about religion. Espionage is another common crime you can be arrested for.

The North Korean regime is known for handing out excessive prison sentences. However, in most cases, prisoners are released well before their sentence is up, thanks to international pressure and diplomatic dealings.

Arrest of Aijalon Gomes

Aijalon Gomes, a 30-year-old from Boston, Massachusetts, was an English teacher in South Korea. On a cold winter's day in 2010, he decided to try the unthinkable; sneak into North Korea. Wanting to offer humanitarian aid to the people of North Korea, Gomes walked across the frozen Tumen River. He was immediately arrested by border guards and sentenced to eight years in prison.

Fortunately, seven months into his sentence, former United States President Jimmy Carter came to the rescue and negotiated Gomes' release. Gomes returned to the United States, where in 2015, he published a memoir based on his experience titled *Violence and Humanity*. Sadly, he committed suicide two years later in San Diego, California.

Arrest of Kenneth Bae

In 2013, Kenneth Bae, another American, spent 735 days in prison in North Korea. While in prison, Bae, a diabetic, became extremely sick and was hospitalized but fortunately survived. In his 2016 book, *Not Forgotten*, Bae describes his life as a prisoner and the countless hours of forced manual labor.

Arrest of Otto Warmbier

One of the most tragic stories involving a foreigner was the case of Otto Warmbier. An American college student, Warmbier was accused of stealing a poster from the Yanggakdo Hotel on New Year's Day 2016. He was sentenced to prison for 15 years but was released after 529 days in June of 2017. Unfortunately, he was unresponsive and died from neurological injuries two days after his return to the United States. Since this unfortunate event, the United States government has banned their citizens from visiting North Korea.

Famine

From 1994 to 1998, North Korea entered its darkest days. The famine, also known as the Arduous March, decimated the population and infrastructure of the country. Official reports of a death count are unavailable; however, experts agree the number of victims exceeded 500,000.

There are several reasons why such a devastating event took place. In December 1991, the Soviet Union officially disbanded. Without the aid of their "big brother", North Korea was reeling in terms of oil and other Soviet energy imports.

Then, in the summer of 1995, floods of biblical proportions hit North Korea. Not only did these floods destroy agriculture, but they also took out grain reserves and important infrastructure. Hydropower plants and coal mines were damaged beyond repair. Rice and corn production, vital pieces of the North Korean diet, fell almost 75 percent.

For a small country with only 20 percent of land arable, the consequences of this were devastating. As a communist country, citizens depended on food rations provided by the government. With no rations to provide, everyone suffered. To eat two meals a day was considered a privilege. Death by starvation was common.

In August of 1995, North Korea made an official request for humanitarian aid. China, along with two of North Korea's biggest "enemies", South Korea and the United States, donated the most food.

While defectors today say that hunger and starvation are still a major problem in North Korea, nothing can compare to the Arduous March of the mid-1990's. Hopefully the people of North Korea will never have to endure another march.

How You Can Help

As an isolated nation, it is extremely difficult to volunteer inside or donate food to North Korea. However, there are several organizations that specialize in helping North Korean refugees get on their feet and enjoy a safe, pleasant life.

Crossing Borders

crossingbordersnk.org

Crossing Borders is a faith-based nonprofit organization that offers assistance to North Korean refugees currently living in China. Since its founding in 2003, Crossing Borders has helped over 1,000 refugees and orphans. You can join their mission by donating, fundraising, or simply spreading the word on the difficulties of being an undocumented North Korean migrant in China.

Liberty in North Korea

libertyinnorthkorea.org

Based in Long Beach, California, Liberty in North Korea (LiNK) has been in existence since 2004. This nonprofit aims to rescue North Koreans currently hiding in China and resettle them to South Korea or the United States. In addition, LiNK also regularly produces videos and holds functions to raise awareness of the atrocities of the government. If you want to help this wonderful organization and its mission, you can donate, fundraise, volunteer, or buy cool gifts, including art prints from Sun Mu, from their online store.

CHAPTER 18

NUCLEAR THREAT

Nuclear weapons are the deadliest weapons on Earth, capable of leveling entire cities in an instant. Only nine countries on the planet currently are equipped with such weapons.

North Korea began building nuclear facilities in the mid 1980's. While there were concerns within the international community, it was widely believed that North Korea lacked the scientists, technology, and resources to develop into a serious threat.

Throughout the 1990's, North Korea turned its nuclear program on and off. When the United States removed weapons from South Korea, North Korea agreed to remove theirs and halt their program. However, testing and manufacturing would continue in secrecy. Amid the devastating famine of the mid 1990's, North Korea again agreed to halt production of their weapons in exchange for United States aid. Again, production began in secret.

As the new millennium arrived, North Korea was declared an enemy by the United States, accused of harboring weapons of mass destruction. In 2003, for the first time, North Korea officially admitted that they did indeed have nuclear weapons and withdrew themselves from the Nuclear Non-Proliferation Treaty.

In 2003, the Six Party Talks were called in Beijing, China. These meetings included members of six countries; North Korea, South Korea, Japan, China, the United States, and Russia. Six meetings were held from 2003 to 2007, and North Korea finally agreed to shut down its main nuclear reactor. All was relatively quiet for the next couple of years, until North Korea again began conducting nuclear tests in 2009.

In February of 2013, North Korea conducted its first nuclear test under new leader Kim Jong-un. Things got riskier in May of 2015 when North Korean officials announced that they had the capacity to strike the United States mainland with a missile, if need be. In December of 2015, they claimed that a hydrogen bomb had been added to their arsenal. A month later, they declared the hydrogen bomb had been successfully tested.

More frightening news came in the summer of 2017. On July 4, North Korean officials announced that they had conducted the first successful test of an intercontinental ballistic missile, capable of reaching anywhere in the world. Weeks later, through the Korean Central News Agency, the North Korean government announced that if the United States were to ever try and remove Jong-un from office, there would be a nuclear strike to the "heart of the U.S.A."

After threatening to launch missiles in the vicinity of Guam, a United States territory, as well as launching missiles near the coast of Japan, tensions escalated to an all-time high. In August of 2017, President Donald Trump warned Jong-un that if there was an attack on any United States territory, North Korea would experience "fire and fury like the world has never seen."

A month later in September, North Korea was testing hydrogen bombs that experts speculated were eight times the strength of the atomic bombs dropped on Japan.

With the rest of the world anxiously waiting, Trump took to his Twitter account to tell Jong-un that his nuclear weapons button was "much bigger and more powerful than his". He then accused Jong-un of being a "little rocket-man". Jong-un, not amused, responded by calling Trump a "dotard". For those who have never heard this term, a dotard is a derogatory name for an elderly person whose physical and mental strength has deteriorated.

Fortunately, a week after this childlike name-calling, cooler heads prevailed. The White House issued a statement saying it would be willing to talk with North Korea. Trump and Jong-un met in Singapore for the first time in June of 2018. While details about a potential nuclear disarmament have not been made public, it is a step in the right direction. The last thing the world needs are more bombs.

CHAPTER 19

WHAT NOT TO DO

You must remember that while in North Korea, you are almost always being monitored. Follow these rules and you should stay out of trouble.

1. Do NOT call North Korea North Korea. Acceptable names are Korea or the Democratic People's Republic of Korea.

2. Do NOT leave your tour group. With the exception of the hotel, you are not allowed to walk alone anywhere in North Korea. If for some reason you get lost from your group, stay put and wait for help to arrive.

3. Do NOT bring in foreign books/movies/music with any religious or political leanings. (**DON'T EVEN BRING THIS GUIDE!**) Possession of anything with even a slight negative opinion towards North Korea can result in jail time or worse.

4. Do NOT take pictures of military personnel or construction without first obtaining permission.

5. Do NOT criticize the North Korean government or living conditions. If you have problems or concerns, for your own safety it is best to wait until you are out of the country to voice these concerns.

6. Do NOT disrespect the leaders. For the most part, this is common sense. Bow when they tell you to bow.

7. Do NOT fold over, throw out, draw on, or crumble any sort of picture with the leader of North Korea's face on it. This can be from a newspaper, book, or pamphlet. Treat every picture of any of the Kims like a million-dollar check.

8. Do NOT chop off the leader's heads! When taking pictures of the leaders, make sure you capture their entire bodies. Zoomed in pictures of the leader's head on a giant statue are forbidden. Crop your photos once you exit the country.

9. Do NOT expect to use your credit card or find an ATM. Bring cash. American dollars, Chinese yuen, and European euros are surprisingly accepted most places. On guided tours, hotels and most restaurants will be prepaid for. Souvenirs, snacks, drinks, as well as services such as spas and haircuts require cash payment. Tips for your guides are not included but highly recommended, whether in the form of cash or gifts.

10. Do NOT drink the water. There have been reports of foreigners being hospitalized from drinking local water. Bottled water is very inexpensive, so to be safe, stock up when you arrive. Iodine tablets are also a good idea if you're planning on being in the country for an extended period of time.

CHAPTER 20

LANGUAGE

Korean is the official language of North Korea. Communicating in a country where your native language isn't spoken can be quite challenging. Knowing the simple words, phrases, and numbers below will help you along your journey.

WORDS

Hello	*ANNYEONG HASEYO*
Thank You	*KAMSA HAMNIDA*
Sorry	*MIAN HAMNIDA*
Water	*MUL*
Dog	*GAE*
Cheers	*CHUKBAE*
Help	*DOUM*
Yes	*YE*
No	*ANI*
Vegetarian	*SUUISA*
Goodbye	*ANNYEONG*
Safe	*ANJEONHAN*
Tired	*PIGONHAN*
Good	*JOH-EUN*
Bad	*NAPPEUN*
Coffee	*KEOPI*
Hotel	*HOTEL*
Money	*DON*
Restaurant	*LESEUTOLANG*
Rocketbone	*LOKES PPYEO*

NUMBERS

1	*HANNA*
2	*DUL*
3	*SET*
4	*NET*
5	*DASOT*
6	*YASOT*
7	*ELGOB*
8	*YADOL*
9	*AHOP*
10	*YEOL*
20	*SEUMUL*
30	*SEOREUN*
40	*MAHEUN*
50	*SWIN*
60	*YESUN*
70	*ILHEUN*
80	*YEODEUN*
90	*AHEUN*
100	*ON*

CHAPTER 21

INSTAGRAM
ACCOUNTS TO
FOLLOW

With social media platforms such as Instagram, travelers can see up-to-the-second pictures, videos, and stories from the Hermit Kingdom. The following Instagram accounts showcase some exceptionally beautiful content.

@everydaydprk

This account shows North Korea in all seasons, through beautiful photos and videos. See the view from the highest overlook at Mount Paektu or from behind the counter of a bar at Pyongyang International Airport.

@libertyinnorthkorea

Liberty in North Korea, a nonprofit organization, profiles photos and stories of defectors reestablishing themselves in their new country.

@krahun

Krahun, a tourism company, has been in North Korea since 1999. Foodies will love their exquisite images of decadent meals.

@simonkoryo

Simon Cockrell, the general manager of Koryo Tours, has been to North Korea over 180 times! With over 1,400 posts on his account, you can live vicariously through his travels, including special events like Joss Stone's performance and the Pyongyang International Film Festival.

@uritours

Uri Tours, one of the leading tour operators in North Korea for over 15 years, posts highlights of their trips throughout their page. See images of ski resorts, dolphin shows, golf courses, orphanages, and other places you might not get the chance to visit.

@erictalmadge

Eric Talmage was the Pyongyang Bureau Chief for the Associated Press. He suffered a heart attack and died while jogging in Japan in May of 2019. With almost 1,200 posts on his account, we can continue to honor and admire his work, particularly his artistic, moving images of North Korea.

@nknewsorg

Hear about current North Korean news stories, as well as many historical posts, on this fascinating profile which partners informative captions with professional-grade photos.

@shaneohodhrain

Shane Horan, a professional photographer from Ireland, has spent years documenting life in the Hermit Kingdom. His photos of water parks, festivals, and school performances are enlightening.

FAREWELL

My trip though North Korea was certainly a life changing experience. It is a country full of interesting people, natural beauty, and a strong sense of national pride.

While nearly every nation on Earth has significantly globalized, North Korea has not. In Paris you can grab a Big Mac at a McDonalds. On the shores of Lake Titicaca in Bolivia you can withdraw money from an ATM cash machine. On the Galapagos Islands, you can walk into a convenience mart and grab an ice-cold refreshing bottle of Coca Cola. In Namche Bazaar, Nepal, in the shadows of Mount Everest, you can connect to a reliable Wi-Fi source and surf the internet or stream your favorite show. In North Korea, none of this is possible.

As a tourist, this allows us to experience the world outside of our comfort zone. It forces us to try new things. It also allows us to appreciate the freedom that we take for granted. Many North Koreans do not even know that free internet exists, or that someone in another country can use their passport to visit almost any country in the world.

Traveling North Korea is a throwback to how traveling was decades ago, when all you had was a guidebook, and I hope this one will help you in your journey to the Hermit Kingdom.

Your friend,

Meet the Author

J.R. JaBone

Rocketbone's Guide to North Korea is JaBone's first book. He traveled to North Korea in November of 2016 and was wowed by the secrets and mysteries of the Hermit Kingdom. When he is not reading books, JaBone enjoys concerts, movies, traveling, bicycling, hiking, and paddle boarding in his hometown of Miami, Florida.

Instagram: @rocketbonebooks

E-Mail: rocketbonebooks@gmail.com

Meet the Illustrator

Zulfikar Rachman

Zulfikar is a Graphic Designer based in Surabaya, East Java, Indonesia. He has enjoyed drawing since childhood and earned a graphic design degree in 2006. His hobbies include watching movies and reading comics. In addition to *Rocketbone*, he has created his own comic book, *the Twilight Chronicles*.

Instagram: @zulfikar.zull

E-Mail: zulfikar.mvl@gmail.com

Thank you...

A special thank you to Susie, Bernie, and Tim for their help in editing *Rocketbone's* first guide.